The
National Parks
and other Wild Places of
Southern Africa

To my wife Wendy, who gave me such enormous
support on our travels in the wild – Nigel Dennis

To Pat, travelling companion, friend and wife, with
love and thanks – Roger de la Harpe

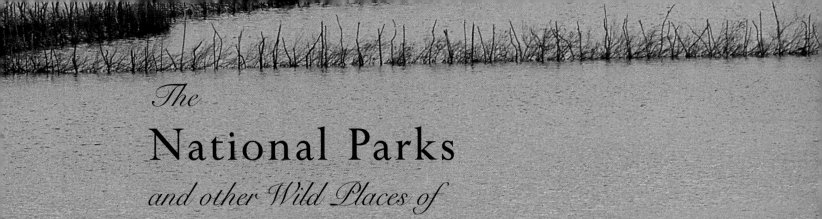

The
National Parks
and other Wild Places of
Southern Africa

PHOTOGRAPHS BY NIGEL DENNIS & ROGER DE LA HARPE

TEXT BY BRIAN JOHNSON BARKER

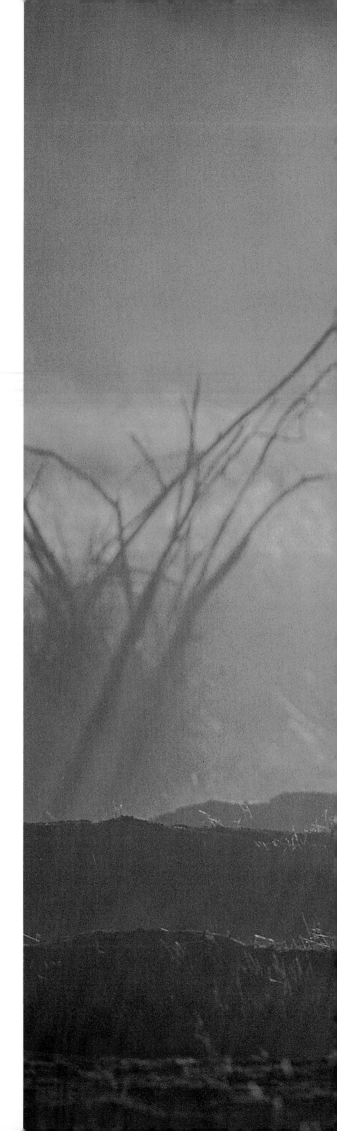

First published in 1999 by New Holland Publishers Ltd
London • Cape Town • Sydney • Auckland
24 Nutford Place, London W1H 6D0, United Kingdom
80 McKenzie Street, Cape Town 8001, South Africa
14 Aquatic Drive, Frenchs Forest, NSW 2086, Australia
218 Lake Road, Northcote, Auckland, New Zealand

2 4 6 8 10 9 7 5 3 1

ISBN - 1 86872 212 0

Project Manager: Pippa Parker
Editor: Peter Joyce
Editorial Assistant: Gisele Raad
Designer: Dominic Robson
Cartography: Eloise Moss
Illustrator: Annette van Zyl

Reproduction by Hirt and Carter (Pty) Ltd, Cape Town

Printed and bound in Singapore by Tien Wah Press (Pte) Ltd

PUBLISHER'S NOTE

For ease of reference by the general reader, species are for the most part referred to by their
common, as opposed to scientific, names throughout this book. Scientific names can be found in
many of the titles listed in the Further Reading section on page 174. In some instances, however,
they have had to be used; in a number of others (where they are likely to prove helpful) both the
common and scientific names are given. The maps published in the book are intended as 'locators'
only; detailed, large-scale maps should be consulted when planning a trip. Although the publishers
have made every effort to ensure that the information contained in this book was correct at the time
of going to press, they accept no responsibility for any loss, injury or inconvenience sustained by any
person using this book.

ACKNOWLEDGMENTS

A great many individuals and organizations helped in one way or another in the preparation of this
book. Photographs taken in South Africa's national conservation areas were done so with the co-operation, and under the supervision, of The South African National Parks. Similar courtesies were offered
by and gratefully accepted from the KwaZulu-Natal Nature Conservation Service. The author, photographers and publisher would like to express their particular indebtedness to the management and staff
of the following:

South Africa: The Cape Peninsula National Park; KwaZulu-Natal Nature Conservation Service;
National Botanic Gardens, Kirstenbosch; Northern Cape Province Nature Conservation Service; Sabi
Sabi Private Game Reserve; The South African National Parks; Springbok Café, Springbok; Western
Cape Department of Nature Conservation. **Namibia**: Ministry of Wildlife, Conservation and Tourism;
Namibia Tourism, Cape Town. **Botswana**: The Department of Wildlife and National Parks. **Zimbabwe**:
The Department of National Parks and Wildlife Management. Special thanks are extended to: Theo
Antoniades (City Lab, Johannesburg), Leon van Rooyen (Namibian Ministry of Wildlife, Conservation
and Tourism), David Daitz (Cape Peninsula National Park), Trevor Dearlove (formerly of The South
African National Parks, Cape Town), Wendy Dennis, Dr George Hughes (KwaZulu-Natal Nature
Conservation Service), Dr Michael Knight (South African National Parks, Kimberley), Ian Michler, Paul
Tingay, Anita Wong (KwaZulu-Natal Nature Conservation Service), and Geoff Wardropper (Terry's
Photoworld, Pietermaritzburg)

Half-title page: A leopard at rest.
Title page: The limpid waters of Kosi Bay, in South Africa's KwaZulu-Natal province.
Opposite: One of the Kalahari's desert-adapted gemsbok.

CONTENTS

INTRODUCTION

Africa has always enchanted the wanderers of the world – the commercial adventurer, the competing imperialist, the intrepid romantic and, especially, the natural scientist in search of knowledge. A magnificent diversity of wildlife, of landscapes and of human cultures, all flourishing in places remote from and often beyond the ken of the Renaissance European, drew a steady stream of visitors to the continent's shores from the late 15th century onwards. Many of them left descriptions, the earliest ones of strange animals (some of them partially or even entirely imaginary), of pristine plains and forests, of hidden cities and of people whose lifestyles were so very different from – simpler it seemed, even nobler than – their own. Later writers were more meticulous in their observations, though their prose remained lyrical enough at times. In the southern Cape, the 18th-century naturalist François le Vaillant recorded 'lofty forests', 'agreeable hills', 'enamelled meads and the most beautiful pastures'. The great explorer and missionary David Livingstone, on his first visit to the Victoria Falls, wrote of a scene so lovely it 'must have been gazed upon by angels in their flight'.

By the time Livingstone set out on the first of his epic journeys though, the subcontinent was well on its way to becoming the world's biggest killing field: by about 1880, professional hunters had slaughtered so many animals that the survivors could barely provide them with a viable living. It then became the turn of the 'sportsman' in quest of trophies or specimens for zoos and museums. Not too long afterwards, and out of sheer necessity, the concept of game preservation and, eventually, of the wider environmental conservation, was developed.

Previous page: An elephant enjoys a sandbath in Namibia's Etosha park.

Opposite: The cold waters of the Mtarazi Falls plunge down precipitous cliffs in the Nyanga area of Zimbabwe's Eastern Highlands.

Above: The bearded vulture, or lammergeier, ranks among southern Africa's larger and rarer birds of prey. It boasts a wingspan of more than 2.5 metres (nearly 9 feet) and, although it feeds mainly on carrion, occasionally preys on small mammals.

The region is blessed with a magnificent natural heritage. South Africa, for instance, occupies less than one per cent of the Earth's land surface but is home to five per cent of its mammal species, eight per cent of its birds and fully 10 per cent of it higher plants. Each of the countries of southern Africa has played its part – often in the face of tremendous difficulties – in preserving its share of this priceless, magical and (in many cases) threatened legacy.

The southern Africa region extends, wedge-like, from the Tropics to almost 35° South, and embraces the Republic of South Africa and those countries that share with it a common border: Namibia, Botswana, Zimbabwe, Mozambique, Lesotho and Swaziland. The eastern seaboards are washed by the warm waters of the Indian Ocean, while the cold Benguela Current of the Atlantic flows north along the west coast. Ocean temperatures and the location of the major mountain ranges have a profound effect on winds and rainfall, which, in turn, have helped regulate the types of habitats and the life forms that occupy them. In many areas, the number of endemics, plants that have adapted to the particular environment, is impressively high. The Cape Peninsula and adjoining Cape Flats, for instance, sustain more botanical species than do the entire British Isles, and as many frog and toad species as there are in the whole of Europe.

The population of the subcontinent is one of the world's most diverse, the human geography recorded in annals spanning about 500 years and an unwritten history that, locally, dates back to the very birth of modern Man. The Khoina, a small group that includes the Bushmen (or San), are thought to be the original inhabitants of southern Africa. They were hunter-gatherers, and thus distinguished, by custom and lifestyle rather than physically, from other sallow-skinned people who appeared later on the scene, communities who raised cattle and who are loosely known as Khoikhoi. The Bantu-speaking people, whose languages are not related to those of the Khoina, began moving south into Zimbabwe and the far northern parts of South Africa perhaps 2,000 years ago, bringing with them the skills of iron-working, animal husbandry and the raising of crops.

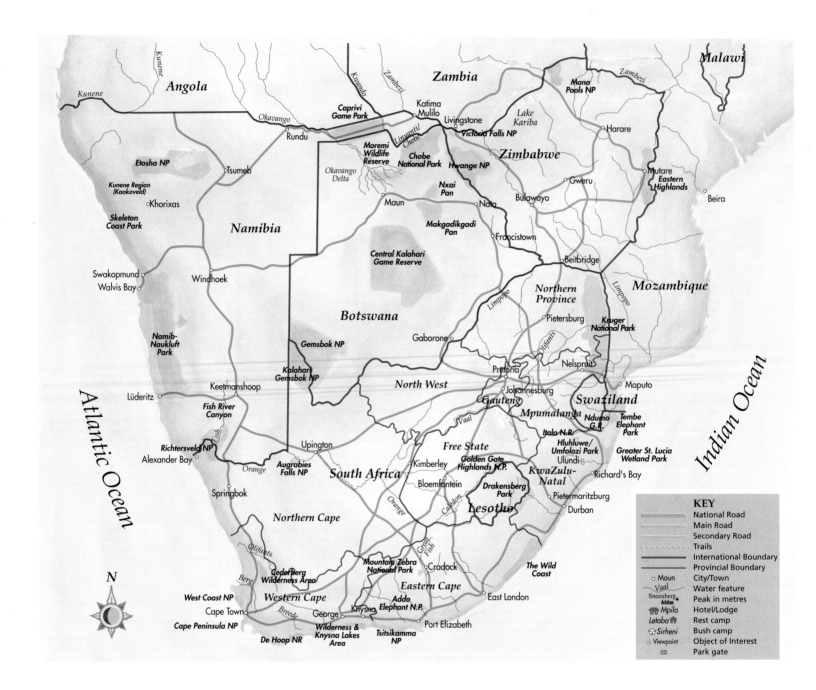

Exploration, trade and conquest brought about both broad divisions and new unions of the Bantu-speakers. They include the Zulu, the Xhosa, the Ndebele, the Sotho, the Venda and the Tsonga of South Africa; the Herero of Namibia; the Shona of Zimbabwe and the Tswana of Botswana. As the new settlement patterns emerged, so Khoina territorial domination waned until these nomads were confined largely to the mountain and desert regions (notably the Kalahari wildernesses) and to parts of Namibia and the present Northern and Western Cape provinces of South Africa.

Expanding European settlement from the mid-17th century, with the attendant arrival of slaves and exiles from the East and from other parts of Africa, added even more complexity to the human equation. It also increased the rate at which agriculture, grazing and permanent settlement encroached upon, and destroyed, the wild kingdom.

The Story of Conservation

The earliest recorded nature-conservation measures were those issued at the Cape of Good Hope in 1655, to prevent the eradication of timber forests at Hout Bay, where pockets of indigenous trees survive to this day. Two decades later there were attempts to conserve wildlife as well, but enforcing the regulations proved too difficult. The most promising measures dated from 1894, when the first game reserve, the Pongola, was proclaimed in the east of what was then the Transvaal Republic (now part of the province of Mpumalanga). Natal's Hluhluwe and Umfolozi game reserves followed in 1897, the year that saw the creation, in the lowveld of the eastern Transvaal, of the Sabie Game Reserve – later to become the famed Kruger National Park.

Big game is found mainly in the northern parts of the subcontinent, from the Etosha drylands in the west, through the Okavango, Moremi and Chobe areas of

Botswana to Zimbabwe's Hhwange Park, the Zambezi River valley and the major reserves – Gonarezhou (also in Zimbabwe) and the Kruger Park – of the eastern escarpment and lowlands. Floral reserves, from the level of national park down to tiny patches prolific in species, are most plentiful in the Western Cape, of which just a corner makes up the smallest and most richly endowed of the world's six botanical 'kingdoms'. Coastal stretches and their marine organisms are protected in many reserves along southern Africa's seaboard. Major scenic reserves – in which wildlife is by no means absent, merely less obvious – include Namibia's Skeleton Coast and Namib-Naukluft (the latter boasts the world's highest sand dunes) and South Africa's Drakensberg and Golden Gate Highlands parks.

The region's reserves and wildernesses, hugely different in character and function though they may be, combine to preserve the essence of the 'real' Africa. But the old threats, and some new ones, continue to preoccupy the conservationists. Most deadly of all is perhaps the encroachment of farmland and the conversion of the natural ground cover to pasture for domestic livestock – a process as rapid as it is well-nigh irreversible. Rural settlements, too, are constantly expanding and laying claim to water and grazing, to game animals needed for meat, and trees for firewood and building material. Poaching – both for illicit commercial gain and as a means of survival – remains a hugely destructive menace; 'collectors' plunder the environment for plants and animals that are fetching increasingly high prices in an illegal but flourishing world market. Mining and industry sometimes strike with powerful effect from a distance, either consuming or polluting precious water supplies upstream of conservation areas.

But there has been some progress in the struggle to preserve the natural legacy. Conservation itself has developed a long way from the mere preservation of game species – as often as not to provide 'sport' for visiting dignitaries – to an integrated approach to the whole environment. And the decision-makers are now fully conscious of the rewards of ecotourism.

Increasingly, the needs of impoverished rural folk are seen as complementary to rather than in conflict with the requirements of tourism. Communities living in or close to reserves, instead of being moved (as happened frequently in the past), remain to help in the task of conservation and, in return, share the rewards generated by the development of lodges and hotels and the growing numbers of ecotourists. Moreover, the creation and administration of reserves, instead of being a purely government responsibility, is rapidly becoming privatized with impressive results in terms of accommodation and specialized safaris. The goodwill and participation of both commerce and the local communities,

Below: The Namib, which lies along and inland from Namibia's Atlantic seaboard, is the world's most ancient desert. Despite its aridness and the searing daytime heat, it sustains a surprising variety of life forms.

Opposite, below: One of the lizards found in South Africa's Cederberg.

not only in southern Africa but also the world over, are signs that human society is at last coming to appreciate the benefits that can be gained from proper management of the Earth's dwindling natural resources.

Parks and Reserves

There are several categories of conservation areas in southern Africa. National parks occupy state-owned land and are created by parliamentary statute and regulated at the level of central government. Other reserves may be controlled at national, provincial or local-authority level, while private reserves of one kind or another are fast growing in number and sophistication.

As a general rule, national parks are given the highest degree of protection, with human activity strictly controlled and exploitation of wildlife (except for the purposes of management) prohibited. A particular category of reserve, the 'game management' or 'safari' area that has evolved in Zimbabwe, may allow controlled trophy hunting. Some private reserves and many game farms also cater for hunters. Fishing (with a restricted 'bag' for consumption only) is sometimes permitted within otherwise tightly monitored areas.

There are literally hundreds of provincial, local and private reserves, many created for very specific purposes – to preserve a fragile vegetation type, for instance, or even a particular species (such as the rare

Below: The saddlebilled is one of southern Africa's eight stork species. It is found in the eastern and northern parts of the region.

Bottom right: Buffalo on the sunlit grasslands of northern KwaZulu-Natal.

Brenton blue butterfly, found near Knysna on the southern coast). There is also a social spin-off: in many instances reserves are geared to draw local communities into their management and organisation and, through this contact, to spread the gospel of conservation. Reserves at all levels offer education-oriented activities – courses for schoolchildren, for example, and wilderness trails for adults. Experienced guides conduct visitors on walking trails through the protected areas, both to ensure their safety and, more positively, to introduce them to the lore of the wild. Most conservation areas also offer shorter, self-guided trails, on which visitors embark armed with a printed description and simple map, enabling them to find their own way around and to identify the wildlife along the route.

The Ways of the Wild

A number of basic rules and conventions should be borne in mind when driving or walking through a reserve. They are designed to ensure the integrity of the habitats while interfering as little as possible with a visitor's enjoyment and freedom of movement, and they include the following:

Everything within a conservation area is protected – animals, birds, insects, trees, flowers, rocks, even natural debris. Fallen branches and animal carcasses, for example, become the busy focus of attention – of insects (in the case of the former) and of scavenging birds and mammals (in the case of the latter) – and should be left to take their place in the rhythm of life.

A wild animal's routines should not be disrupted in any way. In particular, it should never be fed: it could well become accustomed to and

dependent on human handouts, will cease to hunt or forage for itself, and the natural cycle will be irreparably broken. Moreover, it may well become a nuisance or even a danger to visitors and will, in most cases, have to be destroyed.

If you are concerned about something you've seen – an injured buck, perhaps, or an abandoned cub – tell a warden or other park official about it. They will know what action (if any) should be taken. On no account should you attempt to play the bush doctor.

Stay in your vehicle unless you're in a clearly marked 'designated area' – a waterhole, picnic spot or viewpoint. Do not sleep in the open, or even in an open tent, outside an established camp site, most especially if there are lion or spotted hyena in the vicinity.

Don't stray off the beaten track, or try to take short-cuts across country. Getting lost on a back road may lead to trouble and even tragedy. Sticking to the public roads, moreover, helps safeguard micro-habitats, and helps reduce the threat of soil erosion.

Treat the environment and its animals with respect, and with caution. Remember that you are in wild country, and although the game may seem 'tame' in some places, appearances can be dangerously deceptive.

Light fires only in camp, at picnic sites and other appropriate places; don't throw cigarettes (or indeed anything) from the vehicle. Fire is a very real hazard in the veld, and its consequences can be disastrous.

Malaria and bilharzia – a debilitating disease contracted from a water-living snail – are endemic in some parts of southern Africa. Take an anti-malarial course of drugs before entering the affected area; avoid any form of contact with bilharzia-infested water.

There is enormous satisfaction in seeking, finding and identifying some of the myriad species of the southern African wild, whether they be the large and charismatic animals – the 'big five' for instance – or the smaller and less significant (but in their own way just as fascinating) ones, be they reptiles, birds, insects, trees or flowers. The skills are easily learnt if you have the patience to watch, to listen and, most important, to keep still. Secretive creatures, such as the leopard, are only rarely seen, but there is a real sense of achievement in spotting and identifying its paw print close to where impala antelope have trampled the waterhole's mud. Acquire the habit of looking not only down and around, but also of looking up: life in the branches and tree tops is well worth watching. Select a good site (in shade and near a waterhole, for example) and stay there, as still and as quietly as you can. On balance, you will find it far more rewarding, and more relaxing, than chasing through the countryside from one view site to the next.

Game-spotting, though, is only part of the story. In observing the various species, one comes to understand a deeper truth, to embrace a wider vision of the wilderness, its natural balances, its interdependencies, its orderliness. These perceptions bring their own rewards, most especially that rare peace that comes with the realisation that this is how the world was created, and that it is surely worth preserving.

Below: Lionesses at play in the Sabi Sabi Private Game Reserve.

Top right: A blister beetle settles on a sweetthorn twig.

SOUTH AFRICA

The Republic of South Africa occupies the southern portion of the African continent, its 3,000-kilometre (1,800-mile) seaboard running in a vast semi-circle from the cool Atlantic in the west and around the Cape to the warm Indian Ocean in the east, its relatively narrow coastal belt fringed by mountains that are seen at their loftiest and most spectacular in the Drakensberg range of KwaZulu-Natal.

Beyond is the great interior plateau, rising in a series of terraces that includes the semi-arid plains of the Karoo, the prairie-like grasslands of the Middleveld and Highveld and the sandy wastelands of the northwest. Only the far southwestern part of the country, which embraces Cape Town and the lovely winelands of its hinterland, enjoys a Mediterranean type climate, receiving its rains in winter; the rest falls, for the most part, within the summer-rainfall region. That is not to say, though, that the land is well watered. On the contrary, South Africa is one of the world's drier countries: mean annual rainfall is about 450 millimetres (18 inches, or just over half the global average), and there are dramatic regional variations: Port Nolloth in the west averages a pitiful 60 millimetres (2 inches) a year while, in dramatic contrast, the eastern coastal areas are blessed with more than 1,000 millimetres (40 inches). All of which determines the nature of the vegetation – which is extremely varied, ranging from the dense savanna and bush country of the Lowveld, the montane forests of the highlands and the great grassland plains of the eastern interior through the dwarf scrublands of the west to the richly diverse 'fynbos' of the Cape Floral Kingdom.

South Africa is famed for its wildlife heritage, which is at its most prolific and visible in the various protected areas of the northern and eastern regions, several of which are home to the 'big five' of the animal kingdom. Other sanctuaries are more specialized, serving as havens for certain types of often vulnerable, always precious plant, animal or bird life.

Left: The rugged splendour of the Golden Gate Highlands National Park, located in the uplands of the eastern Free State. The high Maluti mountains lie to the south.

Above: A young cheetah twosome peers from dense cover in the privately owned Phinda reserve, northern KwaZulu-Natal.

KRUGER NATIONAL PARK

Majestic Haven of the African Wild

The Kruger, South Africa's premier game sanctuary, occupies some 20,000 square kilometres (7,700 square miles) of low-lying, heat-hazed bushveld in the far northeastern corner of the country – an enormous expanse of savanna, grassland plain and woodland that sustains a breathtaking variety and number of living forms. Indeed it is home to more kinds of animal and bird life than any other conservation area in Africa.

It is also one of the continent's oldest parks, starting life, in a relatively modest way, as the Sabie Game Reserve in 1898. Its first and long-serving chief warden was James Stevenson-Hamilton, who nurtured the area for more than 40 years and gave his nickname, Skukuza, to its main rest camp (the word, in the local language, means 'the shaver', a reference to his ruthless treatment of poachers). Under Stevenson-Hamilton's guidance the park flourished, expanded, achieved national status (in 1926, when it was renamed) and is now majestic home to nearly 150 different mammal species, 510 types of bird and impressive populations of reptiles, amphibians, fish (a surprising 49 species) and countless invertebrates.

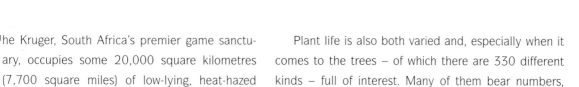

Plant life is also both varied and, especially when it comes to the trees – of which there are 330 different kinds – full of interest. Many of them bear numbers, which enables one to identify species with ease.

In terms of its vegetation the park can be roughly divided into sections. The land southwest of the Olifants River, the midline, is fairly well treed with acacia, marula and combretum, a family that includes the red bushwillow, which has heavily scented, cream-coloured flowers that bloom from September through to February. In the southeast are grassy plains, shaded here and there by knobthorn, that extend into the stunted, butterfly-leafed mopane country of the northeast. Bushwillow and mopane trees, taller than their eastern neighbours, are the dominant species of the northwest quadrant. Quite distinctive from all these are the strips of lush vegetation – embracing, among much else, stands of splendid sycamore figs and Natal mahoganies – that line the Kruger's rivers.

Different, too, is the far northern part of the park, a region of great floral diversity, of many landscapes. This is the meeting place of fully nine of Africa's major ecosystems, and it encompasses a kaleidoscopic variety of habitats – bushveld and wetland, rolling grassland, forest, low woodland, bare granite outcrop, laval flat and deep ravine. The principal

Opposite, top left: Male chacma baboons take their turn at caring for the young.

Opposite, bottom left: The impala, one of the most common – and most graceful – of the Kruger's residents.

Opposite, right: Euphorbias, with their moisture-rich, rubbery stems, flourish in the drier parts of the Kruger.

Top right: The handsome tawny eagle.

Above: The Tsange River in the rainy season. Like many of the Kruger's watercourses, it dries up in the winter months.

Below: Bathing not only keeps the hippo cool but takes a massive weight off its stubby legs.

northern river is the Luvuvhu, a quiet, deep-shaded tropical watercourse girded by stately ebonies, gnarled and liana-festooned figs and groves of ghostly fever trees. Some of the region's myriad living forms are found nowhere else on earth. And it holds human interest as well: Man's long association with this bountiful area is strikingly revealed in Bushman rock paintings and in the archaeological sites of Masorini and Thulamela.

The Big Five

This quintet comprises the large, 'charismatic' animals that every visitor hopes to see in the wild, namely elephant, rhino, buffalo, lion and leopard. They aren't necessarily the biggest or heaviest (though the elephant is champion in both respects), and many other life forms are just as notable in their own way, but each represents a particular quality that humans admire, be it strength, courage, grace, resourcefulness, speed, stamina or sheer beauty.

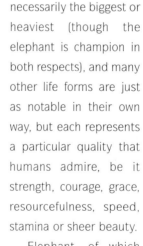

Elephant, of which there are around 8,000 in residence, can be seen throughout the park, most often in groups of about 30 animals and sometimes accustomed enough to the human presence to allow vehicles to approach within a few metres. However, let caution prevail (some animals are easily irritated); move very slowly and keep as still and as quiet as you can. An elephant that turns to face you with raised trunk and flapping ears feels uneasy, and it may be time to move away.

Despite their size (an adult bull weighs more than five tons), these great animals can cover the ground at a surprising speed, although they're too heavy to jump and are easily stopped by low obstacles. They are also good swimmers, and will even, sometimes, walk along the bottom of a lake or river, using their trunk as a breathing tube. Eyesight is good enough only at close range; hearing and sense of smell are acute. A touchingly human-like quality is the elephant's concern for its fellows: orphaned calves are invariably adopted, for instance, and injured and sick animals are supported, even actively helped by the group.

Rhino became regionally extinct some decades ago but reappeared on the scene during the 1960s, when a group of 300 – of the white kind – were brought in from Zululand. Since then the population has flourished. The black rhino has also been reintroduced.

The common names tend to be somewhat confusing. 'White' does not relate to the colour; rather, it is either a corruption of the Dutch-Afrikaans word 'wyd', a

and vengefulness when provoked or wounded. Hunters are especially wary of them: they have been known to double back on their tracks to lie in ambush for their pursuers. When threatened by predators, notably lions, bulls will form a defensive ring, or laager, around the cows and calves. The animals usually congregate in herds of up 200 and more, but small groups and solitary bulls, perhaps exiled from the group after losing a mating battle (these are the most dangerous of the species), may also be encountered. The herds are most often seen grazing in the cooliness of early morning and late afternoon (they also feed at night), preferring to lie up in the shade of thick bush during the heat of day. Like elephant and rhino, buffalo tend to stay fairly close to, and like to wallow in, water.

The Kruger is home to around 1,500 lions, most of which live in prides of half a dozen or so individuals (though groups of up to 40 have been observed) in the central and south – areas rich in the zebra and wildebeest that comprise much of their diet. The full-grown male is universally recognized as the lord of the veld, the 'king of beasts', but this regal status is somewhat belied by the animal's lifestyle: the leader of a pride tends to be indolent, sleeping and eating his way through most of the day; his females and, to a lesser extent, the younger animals do most of the hard work involved in stalking and catching prey.

Left: This warthog, characteristically, kneels as it forages, uprooting tasty bulbs and other tubers with snout and tusks.

Above: The imperious bateleur, seen here at rest. The handsome bird spends much of its day effortlessly gliding and soaring.

reference to the wide, square-lipped mouth of the grass-eating animal, or 'wydende', which means 'grazing'. The two species can quite easily be distinguished: the black rhino is the smaller of the two (850 kilograms/ 1,870 pounds, as opposed to its cousin's hefty 2,200 kilograms/4,900 pounds), has a pointed upper lip adapted for grasping twigs and leaves (that is, for browsing), carries its head higher, and is the more agile of the two, less predictable, more highly strung and irritable. Moreover, a black rhino calf will walk or trot behind its mother, the white rhino calf stays in front of her.

Placid, inquisitive and remarkably like domestic cattle: these are one's immediate impressions of the African buffalo. But the animals, with their massive curved horns, have an ominous reputation for cunning

Left: Close contact is part of the greeting ceremony between two mature elephant bulls in the Sabi Sabi reserve.

Previous pages: A pride of lions, fed, watered and relaxed, has time for play on a fallen tree.

Right: The wild dog looks disarmingly domesticated, but is in fact only distantly related to the household pet. It is a restless, nomadic traveller and a superbly accomplished pack hunter.

The typical lion hunt, in fact, is a masterly exercise in teamwork: the dominant male needs do little more than show himself to start a panicky flight of an antelope herd straight into the teeth and claws of the strategically positioned lionesses. But the majesty is there, never more in evidence than when the lion is called on to defend the pride or his territory. He is immensely powerful, capable of breaking the neck of a large antelope with a single blow of his huge forepaw, and of carrying the equivalent of his own weight in his jaws, and astonishingly quick across the ground. Contrary to popular belief he can also climb trees, and is an excellent swimmer.

Above: The impala lily, also known as the Sabie star, decorates the Kruger's broad acres in winter.

Second of the Kruger's big cats is the leopard, a shy, secretive, nocturnal, superbly adaptable and breathtakingly handsome creature that, unlike the lion, is solitary in its habits – for the most part: a female and her cubs may stay together for almost two years while the young learn the hunting craft. Up to three (occasionally more) cubs may be born in a litter. This animal, too, is immensely strong, able not merely to carry prey equivalent to its own body weight but clear a three-metre (ten-foot) high obstacle with the carcass in

its jaws. More often, though, it will haul its kill high up into the branch of a tree, well out of reach of hyaenas, jackals and other determined scavengers, to cache the remains for later consumption.

The leopard's coat, with its solid dark spots on the limbs and 'rosettes' on the body, provides perfect camouflage. The animal is not easily detected: during the daylight hours it hides away in thick bush or among the rocky outcrops, well out of sight, but can occasionally be seen basking in the early morning sun close to its lair, which may be a crevice, cave or an old aardvark burrow.

Wildlife Parade

The big five are prominent species, much sought after and photographed by visitors, but they represent just a tiny fraction of the Kruger's wildlife complement. Among other large predators are the cheetah, fastest and perhaps most graceful of all hunters; the endangered wild dog; the brown and spotted hyaenas, and the attractive little black-backed jackal.

And then there are the herbivores, among them stately giraffe, plains zebra, blue wildebeest, roan, kudu, eland and waterbuck. An especially familiar sight are the impala, so common that they become something of a fixture on the landscape and one tends to pass them by. These medium-sized, delicate-looking, gentle-eyed antelope, though, are well worth more than a passing glance: when disturbed, the animals will take off across the veld in a series of dramatic, three-metre (ten-foot) high leaps, the whole group bounding, weaving and swerving through the bush in unison to create a wonderfully elegant, ballet-like spectacle.

Most of the Kruger's animals can be found throughout the park, but each has its preference for particular areas. Roan, tsessebe and eland, along with the elephant, tend to prefer the mopane scrublands of the north; the southern parts are favoured by black rhino, white rhino (especially in the southwest), blue wildebeest, giraffe and zebra; bushbuck and the handsome, shaggy-coated nyala seek the cover of riverine forest; buffalo, kudu, sable, waterbuck, the abundant impala, baboon and vervet monkey are everywhere.

Some of the smaller antelope, such as grysbok, duiker and steenbok, are elusive, seen only when they break cover. Crocodile and hippo have their favourite areas, but to a greater or lesser extent are likely to be found along the reaches of any watercourse or dam. The Kruger's many different habitats attract a huge diversity of birds – more than 500 different species altogether.

The raptors are special, and highly visible as they hunt over and scavenge on the teeming veld, but there's much more to discover and observe beyond the limits of the obvious – in the woodlands and forests (which are home to the shy and colourful Knysna lourie and a variety of parrots) and along the watercourses. It is the birds of prey, however, that provide the drama; an especially memorable sight is the frenzy of voracious, noisy white-backed vultures as they gather at a carcass. They are invariably joined by the rarer Cape vulture and the lappet-faced vulture (both of them much larger than the whitebacked) and by the spindly-legged marabou stork. The rest camps, because of their proximity to water – all are sited close to river or dam – are ideal bird-watching areas; the watercourses of the northern and southwestern parts are especially rewarding.

Above: One of the Kruger's white rhinos slakes its thirst while an elegant impala, with more to fear, warily approaches the water.

Left: Safety in numbers: if disturbed, these impala antelope will bound away across the veld in a series of huge, ballet-like leaps.

Below: The kori bustard is among the world's heaviest flying birds.

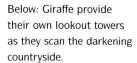

Below: Giraffe provide their own lookout towers as they scan the darkening countryside.

Getting Around

The Kruger attracts close on a million visitors a year, and is superbly equipped to do so – in terms of both accommodation and travel. It boasts an extensive (but surprisingly unobtrusive), 2,600-kilometre (1,600-mile) network of roads, some of them tarred, the lesser ones gravelled, that link the 20-plus rest camps to each other and to a splendid variety of waterholes, viewsites and picnic spots. Speed limits are strict, and closely monitored, to protect both the motorist and the animals – which often appear suddenly on the road, seemingly out of nowhere. In any event, there is absolutely no point in driving quickly because you won't see much. Once outside the rest camps, you may not leave your vehicle except at picnic sites and other designated places, and even at these you alight at your own risk.

But in reality a drive, however leisurely, is usually less rewarding than keeping vigil at a waterhole, especially in the dry months. Wait quietly there and, with a little patience, you're almost certain to see something of interest, perhaps smaller creatures at first, but the larger and even the rare animals will arrive at some time to drink. Two of the most attractive viewing points are at the Orpen and Mlondozi dams.

For those with time to spare and a wish for more intimate encounters with the African wild, there are the various wilderness trails, ranger-led foot safaris designed not as a physical challenge but to stimulate the mind and the eye. Trailists overnight in simple, A-frame huts;

Left: The Kruger landscape at the magical sunset hour.

Below: The African buffalo, which closely resembles domestic cattle in size and build, is peaceful enough if left alone.

sociable evenings around the campfire, with the sounds of the bushveld night all around, are times that will linger in the memory. As compelling in its own way is the night drive, when you can listen to and watch (by the light of a spotlight) some of the animals that are rarely seen by day. Experienced rangers also conduct special day-time bush drives – part of an educational service based on Skukuza, Berg-en-Dal and Letaba rest camps – which enable groups to visit parts of the park that are normally out of bounds. These are popular excursions, and to make sure of a place one has to book oneself on them a good two months in advance.

Staying There

The Kruger National Park has been called 'South Africa's biggest hotel', and even likened to a glorified zoo, but the comparisons are both odious and invalid. At any one time it may, admittedly, be hosting up to 5,000 people (many of whom are day visitors) but the infrastructure that has been designed for this massive human presence – the rest camps, the roads and the 'visual bands' along either side of them, the picnic spots, viewsites and other designated areas – account for less than three percent of the park. The rest is wild Africa.

There are 13 major public camps, half a dozen or so smaller, exclusive ones (for groups) and five bushveld camps, which are small, comfortable, and somewhat remote. The latter are suited to the more casual, get-away-from-it-all visitor.

Above: This bushbuck ewe is one of a solitary and nocturnal species, rarely seen by day.

Right: A mature male leopard finds security and comfort in the fork of a large tree.

The bigger camps are spaciously laid out, firmly fenced for security, most of them graced by trim lawns, flowering plants and stately indigenous shade trees. Each has its pleasantly informal restaurant, strategically sited to overlook river or game-rich valley; its shop, its information centre; its camping-caravanning ground, and its bungalows and huts, most of which are airconditioned. Some venues have a more extensive range of facilities than others; Skukuza, the 'capital' of the Kruger, is not so much a rest camp as a bustling little village complete with supermarket, restaurants, post office, bank, doctor's surgery, motor workshop, library, exhibition hall and busy little airport.

At the top of a camp's accommodation range are the 'guest houses', secluded, well-appointed, often privately owned and run units that sleeps six to nine people (the main bedroom with en-suite bathroom) and a fully equipped kitchen. Smaller guest cottages, also with two bathrooms, are available in most rest camps.

A typical 'family cottage' has two two-bed rooms, bathroom, toilet, kitchen and a veranda enclosed with insect-proof gauze. An ordinary cottage has one bedroom, a living room and bathroom, and a partially equipped kitchen. Bungalows have one room, a bathroom, and a kitchenette (some units share kitchen facilities). More basic huts are also available.

The Private Reserves

Sprawling across the bushveld countryside to the west of the Kruger park are some of Africa's largest privately owned game reserves. No fences separate them; nor are there any barriers between them and the Kruger, so the animals are free to wander at will.

Each of these reserves comprise a number of farms and game properties, some of whose owners have combined to establish commercial lodges that cater for the more prosperous end of the tourist market, and which are noted for the luxury of their accommodation, the cuisine they offer, the personal attention the rangers lavish on their guests and the high concentrations of game (including the 'big five') in their areas. Some of the lodges, among them Londolozi (famed for its leopards), Mala Mala, Motswari and M'Bali, Tanda Tula, Sabi Sabi and Ngala, are now as internationally respected as Kenya's famed Treetops.

Guests of the private lodges enjoy the ultimate in safari experiences. A warm summer's day may start at

Left: Bateleur bushveld camp offers self-catering cottages on the Shingwedzi River, in the Kruger's wilder northern parts. This is renowned tusker country.

5.30 am with tea or coffee, followed by a game-spotting drive in a 4x4 manned by a ranger and a tracker. Breakfast is enjoyed either in the bush or back at camp. As the temperature begins to rise, encouraging both man and animal to conserve energy, one retires to the coolness of lounge, pool or chalet, though there's also the option of a gentle guided walk or a spell in a comfortable observation hide. Lunch is a pleasant affair taken either inside or on the shady terrace, followed by more quiet time until the afternoon game drive, which continues until just before sunset. The group then returns to camp for dinner, perhaps eaten around a log fire in the 'boma' – an outdoor enclosure sheltered by a screen of tall reeds. The evening meal is a sociable affair; diners may enjoy a 'cabaret' of traditional singers and dancers, and the meal often turns into an exuberant party. Alternatively, a night drive might be laid on.

The Timbavati reserve is perhaps best known for its white lions, first seen in 1959 and the object of international interest when four cubs were born (three here, one at Tshokwane in the Kruger park) in the 1970s. Several more have since made their appearance and all, as far as can be determined, have normally pigmented brothers and sisters. The animals do not represent a new species: the whiteness of the coat is merely the product of a recessive gene.

Below: Loose-limbed and lightning fast, the cheetah is a spectacular hunter, but finds it hard to compete with other large carnivores.

HLUHLUWE-UMFOLOZI PARK

A Safe Refuge for the Endangered Rhino

The green hills of the old Zulu kingdom rise from the sweetly grassed plains where morning mists are scattered by the early sun. It is a landscape that is startlingly beautiful, a compound of grassland, wooded hillsides, forest, dense thicket, savanna, meandering river and lush floodplain fed by (usually) good rains and warmed by the subtropical sun. Add an unrivalled variety of wildlife, and it assumes a magical quality. Once, this was the hunting preserve of kings; the regal grandeur remains.

The presence of so many animals and the pristine nature of their habitats represent something of an ecological miracle. The area was originally set aside as the Hluhluwe and Umfolozi game reserves in 1895 (they were among southern Africa's first conservation projects), and for a while they served their purpose admirably, sustaining huge game populations. Human encroachment, in the early days, posed little threat: farmers and ranchers stayed clear, kept at bay by the tiny and deadly tsetse fly, an insect that has little effect on wild mammals (though they may become carriers) but infects domestic cattle with nagana, a wasting disease, and humans with sleeping sickness. During the 1920s, however, a massive campaign was launched to eradicate the tsetse fly – by eliminating its host. Thousands of head of game were slaughtered. Happily, more benevolent, chemical means of control were eventually developed (they were first used in 1945); the herds stabilized, and the reserves and their residents staged a remarkable recovery. Now joined together, the Hluhluwe and Umfolozi reserves provide a 96,000-hectare (37,000-square mile) home to healthy populations of herbivores, to their attendant predators, and to a quite magnificent array of birds.

The park lies on an extension of northern KwaZulu-Natal's bushveld plains, hugged in the northwest by the Drakensberg foothills. The Drakensberg is South Africa's most prominent range (see p.50), and it is important to the Hluhluwe-Umfolozi for the rain it wrings from the moisture-laden winds that blow in from the Indian Ocean. The area's major watercourses are the White and Black Mfolozi rivers – a name that translates roughly as 'zigzag' and refers to their convoluted courses – and the Hluhluwe River. Hluhluwe is the local name for the thorny liana or monkey rope (*Dalbergia armata*) that drapes the flanking forests.

The Hluhluwe-Umfolozi Park embraces a wide variety of habitats, which explains its extraordinary wildlife diversity. Much of the countryside, though, is typical acacia-studded savanna grassland, with rich grazing and ample water in a climate that varies from hot to rarely less than warm. Only on the higher ground to the north

Opposite: Both the black and the white rhino were bred back from the edge of extinction on the rolling hills of the Hluhluwe-Umfolozi Park.

Top right: The sycamore fig, a gnarled giant of the riverine forest, grows along the park's watercourses; both the leaves and the fruit have a high nutritive value.

Location: The park lies in northern KwaZulu-Natal, 300 km (185 miles) northeast of Durban.

Climate: Summers are hot, winters mild to cool with occasional cold spells at higher altitudes.

When to go: At any time of the year, but the drier months are the best for game viewing.

Getting there: Driving from the south on the N2: turn left onto the R618 opposite Mtubatuba for Hlabisa/Nongoma. Driving from the north: turn from the N2 opposite Hluhluwe village for the Memorial Gate, or take the R618 opposite Mtubatuba to reach Nyalazi Gate.

Facilities: Information centre, bush camps, chalets (some with staff in attendance); field rangers available. Picnic spots, game-viewing sites, guided walks, game-viewing drives, hiking trails, self-guided walks and auto trails have been laid out. The Hluhluwe section's excellent Hilltop Camp has a restaurant, bar, shop and superette. Petrol is available during set hours.

Wildlife: An impressive variety, including white and black rhino, elephant, buffalo, lion, leopard, giraffe, a wide diversity of antelope and over 300 bird species. Game-viewing hides at waterholes offer visitors close encounters with the wildlife. Be sure to return to your camp by the stated time.

Activities: Game viewing is the main attraction; also bird-spotting and walking/hiking. All-weather roads follow a number of scenic routes, with vistas to the distant Indian Ocean.

Permits and reservations: Book accommodation well in advance through the KwaZulu-Natal Nature Conservation Service (see page 174).

Precautions: Against malaria.

could the temperature ever be described as 'cold' and, even then, only occasionally. Among the rarer habitats is the Mbhombe forest, known for its great strangler figs, its lianas, its milk plums and the white stinkwoods that, according to local tradition, provide protection against the power of witchcraft.

The Big Six – and Others

It is a matter of pride for the park that it provides a safe haven for the 'big six' (as opposed to the more usual 'big five') – elephant, buffalo, lion, leopard and, most notably, black rhino and white rhino.

It was here, in the park's Umfolozi section, that rhino conservation was pioneered while, elsewhere in Africa, poachers relentlessly drove these massive but vulnerable beasts towards extinction. It was here, too (in the 1960s), that the scientists and rangers of the Natal Parks Board perfected drug-darting techniques to capture and move the animals so that breeding herds could be established in other and often distant reserves. Today, Hluhluwe-Umfolozi is home to the world's greatest concentration of the animals – some 1,550 of the white species and 420 of the black wander the park's sunlit spaces.

You will try in vain to identify rhino by colour: the popular names are more or less meaningless. Both species are a muddy grey. The white, though, is more likely to be found in the well-grassed savanna areas, black rhino in the more heavily wooded parts.

The park's big six share their magnificent environment with cheetah, wild dog, spotted hyaena, wildebeest, zebra, giraffe, and large numbers of antelope, ranging from the lordly kudu through the handsome nyala to the shy and tiny duiker,

as well as many types of smaller mammal. Crocodiles, monitors (or leguaans – giant iguana-like reptiles) and hippos are a familiar sight in and around the rivers. The attractive glossy-coated samango monkey can be seen, often in family groups, in the dense riverine forests.

One notable creature, which is also found close to water, is the beautiful and powerful African python, member of a family that comprises the longest snakes in the world. This species sometimes reaches six metres (about 20 feet) in length. Other reptiles found here include the black mamba and the green mamba, both of them deadly in attack but shy (they will move away when they sense a human) and therefore seldom seen.

Bird life is plentiful, and includes the bateleur, a short-tailed, eagle-like raptor that is often seen gliding and soaring with scarcely a movement of its broad wings to keep it aloft. Hlaza, near Hilltop Camp, is reckoned to be the best spot for observing birds of prey, among them the tawny eagle and jackal buzzard. A less-frequent flier is the ground hornbill, whose deep, booming call is one of the classic sounds of the region. Somewhat reminiscent of a black turkey, this large bird spends its day stalking about on the lookout for food, which may be a small tortoise or mammal, snake, frog or any other creature that can be swallowed whole. Among common water-related birds of the area are the African fish eagle, the strange-looking hamerkop, the green-backed heron and the pied and malachite kingfishers.

Above: The black rhino, smaller and more aggressive than its white cousin.

Right: The kudu is a browser, subsisting largely on the leaves and pods of trees and shrubs.

Below: Seeds of the boerboon have been a source of food for man since prehistoric times.

Staying There

The park's headquarters, and its main reception centre,
are located at the fine and fairly new Hilltop Camp in the
Hluhluwe section. The place, beautifully designed, is set
atop a wooded hill, and the vistas from its precincts are
memorable. The view to the east extends to the hazy
blue line of the sea, some 50 kilometres (30 miles)
distant. The amenities are extensive and excellent; an
attractive introduction programme – walks, talks and
video displays – is laid on for visitors.

Hilltop Camp's accommodation ranges from two-bed
rondavels (round huts), with communal bathroom and
kitchen, to four-bed, self-contained chalets. The camp's
Mtwazi Lodge offers luxurious exclusivity; Muntulu and
Munywaneni are pleasant river-bank bush lodges.

The Umfolozi section is also well endowed with
accommodation. Mpila and Masinda are largish rest
camps; the Sontuli and Nselweni bush camps and
Gqoyena and Hlathikhulu bush lodges are beautifully
set on the banks of the Black Mfolozi River; each of
them enjoys pleasant views. A study of the comprehensive horn collection at Mpila will help you to identify
species you meet later on. Hilltop is the only camp at
which you can buy general provisions, and the only one
with a restaurant and bar.

Getting Around

Daily guided walks and night drives start from Hilltop
and Mpila camps. There are also several short, self-
guided trails. Early morning and late afternoon are the
best times to set out: the weather is relatively cool and
these are the hours when the animals, which tend to hide
up in the heat of the day, are most likely to be seen.

Self-guided auto trails provide an introduction to the
natural history of the reserve and the way in which it is
managed. Stop your car at one of the shady picnic sites,
switch off, open the windows and the car becomes a
hide from which you can see and hear, all around you, a
true African wilderness. Guided game-viewing drives,

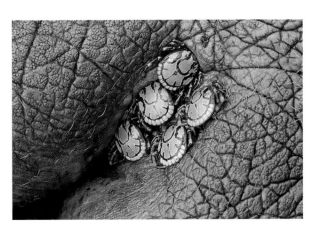

Above: The kurrichane
thrush, a melodious tree-
dweller that finds most of
its food on the ground.

Left: The variegated or
'bont' tick causes disease
in both domestic and wild
animals. The female tick
may lay as many as
20,000 eggs at a time.

Opposite: The dense vegetation along the Mansiya stream in Hluhluwe-Umfolozi provides safe shelter for a wide variety of birds and small mammals.

Right: The sociable little vervet monkey is as much at home on the ground as in a tree.

both during the daylight hours and at night, offer especially rewarding excursions – they usually reveal far more than you would see on your own. Among the best spots for game watching are Hidli Vlei, the areas around Munyawaneni and Muntulu, and the road between Seme and Gunjaneni. You may only leave your vehicle in the designated spots (picnic sites, watering holes, viewing points, all of which are quite clearly marked). The rule ensures your safety: this is wild country, and although the animals may seem placid enough, and even 'tame', appearances can be deceptive: that lazy lion basking at the roadside can spring to lethal life in a split second.

Above: The leopard tortoise, also known as the mountain tortoise, is the largest of the southern African species.

Right: Giraffe mother and calf. This graceful animal's major predator is the lion.

The three-day, four-night Umfolozi Wilderness Trails operate from the beginning of March to the end of November. They do not conform to predetermined itineraries; a trail leader will select the route so that the group approaches game from downwind. Hikers will cover anything up to 12 kilometres (7½ miles) a day and, although the pace is adjusted to suit members of the group, one needs to be in reasonably good physical condition to take part.

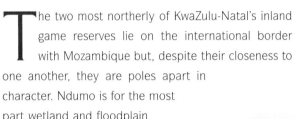

NDUMO AND TEMBE

Twins of the Tropical North

The two most northerly of KwaZulu-Natal's inland game reserves lie on the international border with Mozambique but, despite their closeness to one another, they are poles apart in character. Ndumo is for the most part wetland and floodplain while Tembe, less than six kilometres (under four miles) to the east, mainly comprises dry sand forest. The wildlife profiles are different, too: Ndumo is renowned for its birds, its trees and its fish; Tembe was created in an attempt to conserve the remnant of the region's once prolific free-ranging elephants.

The Watery World of Ndumo

Ndumo is small, its 10,000-hectare (38-square mile) wetlands a delicately laced pattern of lake, stream, floodplain, marshland and reedbed watched over by the grotesquely twisted shapes of giant sycamore figs. Fever trees, named for their association with malaria-infested areas, grow close to the edges of pans and channels and, in serried rows, stand sentinel at Nyamithi Pan. The latter, some four kilometres (2½ miles) in length, is a favourite haunt of hippo and crocodile.

Opposite: Hippo wallow in limpid waters that reflect fever trees, thorny members of the acacia family wreathed in myth: they were once thought to give off a vapour that caused malaria. The disease's name, indeed, derives from the Italian for 'bad air'.

Top right: The 'horns' of this long-horned beetle are really its antennae. Most of southern Africa's 800 species of the beetle are wood-borers.

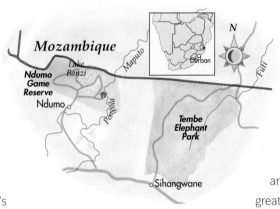

Bright water lilies decorate the even larger Banzi Pan to the north, a place where a myraid aquatic birds gather to breed, among them stork, sandpiper, duck, heron, kingfisher and flamingo. Here, too, you'll find Pel's fishing owl and the imperious African fish eagle. In all, about 420 species of bird have been identified within the Ndumo reserve – which is close in number to those recorded in the Kruger National Park, an area almost 200 times greater in size.

In the far northeast, the sycamore figs grow in dense forests within a wild, ecologically fragile area to which access is strictly controlled. The shaggy-coated nyala, an antelope that fleetingly resembles a young kudu bull, is at home here despite the almost impenetrable nature of the vegetation. Farther away from the pans and the rivers, the drier countryside sustains acacias, grasses and woody shrubs that provide a variety of habitats – as well as food – for white and black rhino, giraffe, buffalo, impala, reedbuck and the rare suni. This last, a tiny antelope (the male weighs a bare five kilograms, or 11 pounds) inhabits the densest thickets, and is independent of water, deriving all its moisture from grazing.

The attraction of Ndumo lies in its bird life and scenery, but guided game walks and drives reveal a surprising amount of wildlife that would otherwise pass largely unnoticed in the fairly dense cover. The self-guided drives are also rewarding. Several excellent viewing hides have been established.

Location: Ndumo and Tembe are in the far northeast of KwaZulu-Natal, and some way inland.

Climate: Summers are hot, often very humid; February is the hottest month. Winters are mild, July the coolest month.

When to go: At any time of the year; each season has its drawcards; the winter months are probably the best for game viewing.

Getting there: From the main N2 highway between Pongola and Mkuze: take the road through Jozini and follow the signposts.

Facilities: Ndumo has a rest camp with communal ablution block and shared cooking facilities, though meals can be prepared by a resident cook. The privately run, fully catered wilderness camp has a dining room adjoining bar, lounge and swimming pool. On offer in Ndumo are conducted 4x4 game-viewing drives and guided bird-watching excursions. Tembe's only overnight facility is a private, fully catered rustic camp; on offer are conducted game drives. A 4x4 is essential for getting around Tembe.

Wildlife: Ndumo is renowned for its bird life, but both reserves have a great variety of large mammals. Tembe is noted for its elephants and, interestingly, for its butterflies.

Permits and reservations: Public accommodation must be booked well in advance through the KwaZulu-Natal Nature Conservation Service (see page 174). For accommodation at Tembe's private tented camp, contact Tembe Safaris on (031) 202 9090; fax 202 8026. Only six parties of day visitors (who must have the use of 4x4 vehicles) are admitted to the park each day.

Precautions: Bilharzia is prevalent; take precautions against malaria, especially in wet weather.

Below: A Nile crocodile shows off its profile. The giant reptile is awkward on land, but extremely proficient in the water.

Bottom left: The goliath heron is frequently seen standing motionless in the water, waiting for a fish or frog to come within striking range of its large, sharp bill.

Bottom centre: The yellow-billed stork, common in the subcontinent's northern wetlands.

Bottom right: The little egret, often seen close to shore in shallow waters, is distinguished from other members of its family by its black legs and yellow feet.

Tembe Elephant Park

For uncounted generations the elephants of Mozambique's coastal plain followed the ancient migratory routes into the Maputaland region of northern KwaZulu-Natal – until fairly recently, when civil war, poaching and growing human concentrations took a heavy toll on the herds. In the late 1980s, however, it was decided (as the lesser of two evils) to erect an electrified fence along the border, and the relatively few elephants which had survived the onslaught are now protected within the 30,000-hectare (120-square mile) reserve. Happily, their numbers have been slowly and steadily increasing – a signal success for conservation.

It is hoped that, one day soon, it may again be safe for elephant to wander freely, for the timeless urge to migrate remains as strong as ever (perhaps the most remarkable example of the imperative occurred in Zimbabwe in 1982, when two elephants swam and waded 40 kilometres (25 miles) across Lake Kariba in a marathon effort lasting 30 hours). The proposed removal of Tembe's northern fences might be part of a general move, in southern Africa, towards trans-border conservation, a programme that could, at some time in the future, see animals of all kinds make their way along 'safe' corridors from one side of the subcontinent to the other. Locally, it is hoped to unite Tembe and Ndumo to form a single conservation unit, and perhaps to add a 54,000-hectare (210-square mile) strip linking the area to Kosi Bay, a series of limpid, bird-rich and beautiful coastal lakes to the east. The combined area would be managed as what is known as a biosphere reserve.

Tembe is known principally for its elephants, but in fact has a lot more to offer. Among other things, it is home to the largest concentration of the shy suni antelope in southern Africa, as well as to white and black rhino, giraffe, nyala, kudu, impala, blue wildebeest,

Left: Elephants form strong group and family bonds that are revealed both under threat and often in moments of quiet, intimate contact.

waterbuck, zebra and many smaller species. Among predators are leopard, hyaena and side-striped jackal. warthog and bushpig are also in residence. The former are the more visible; bushpig, which are more like the domestic pig, tend to lie up in thick shelter during the day, emerging only after nightfall to search for the insects, roots, fruit, eggs, small animals and carrion that comprise their catholic diet. Bird life is brisk, and few visitors fail to be impressed by the number and variety of the area's butterflies. These include the largest South African species, the emperor swallowtail, the rarer Natal swallowtail, and the remarkably variable mocker swallowtail, which may resemble other species.

Getting Around

Much of Tembe's terrain is very sandy, negotiable only by four-wheel-drive (though visitors without a 4x4 can make arrangements with a private tour operator). Ndumo's options include guided walks, game viewing (in open 4x4 vehicles) and bird-watching expeditions. Some of Ndumo's game-viewing roads are also open for self-drive excursions; an unusually rewarding auto trail has been developed.

Staying There

Tembe has a rustic, privately run tented camp that can accommodate up to ten people. Ndumo's rest camp comprises seven three-bed huts with communal kitchen-dining and ablution facilities. A private wilderness camp at Banzi Pan (eight twin-bed tents) offers luxurious accommodation and close encounters with resident wildlife.

Below: The giraffe is at its most vulnerable as it stoops to drink. Fleetness of foot and a lethal kick are its main defences.

GREATER ST LUCIA WETLAND PARK

Maputaland's Magical World of Water

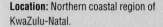

Location: Northern coastal region of KwaZulu-Natal.

Climate: Summers are very hot and humid; winters pleasantly mild.

When to go: At any time of the year, though high summer (January–February) can be uncomfortable.

Getting there: To reach Mkuzi, turn from the N2 about 35 km (22 miles) north of Hluhluwe village and follow the signs. For Cape Vidal, Mapelane and St Lucia Estuary, turn off the N2 at Mtubatuba. Lake Sibaya is accessible through Sodwana Bay.

Facilities: Hotel and private accommodation; shops at St Lucia Estuary; swimming pools at some camps; boats for hire; camp shops; fuel; self-guided walking trails, guided wilderness trails; launch trips and lake cruises.

Wildlife: Loggerhead turtles come ashore on summer nights. Some 400 bird species have been recorded; mammals include the rare suni. Mkuzi is a haven for elephant, rhino, giraffe, leopard, and cheetah, antelope and other small mammals.

Activities: Game-viewing; bird-spotting; turtle-watching (tours during December and January); whale- and dolphin-spotting at Cape Vidal. Many short walks and trails offer visitors the ideal way of exploring and appreciating the environment.. Boating and canoeing on the lake. Fishing is popular; scuba diving and bathing are permitted in selected areas along the coast..

Permits and reservations: Book accommodation well in advance through the KwaZulu-Natal Nature Conservation Service (see page 174).

Precautions: Take the standard precautions against malaria and bilharzia. Be wary of crocodiles and hippo and, in the forests, the placid but highly venomous gaboon viper.

The coastal plateau and seaboard of northern KwaZulu-Natal is known as Maputaland, a fragile, humid, well-watered, low-lying plain that embraces a quite remarkable variety of plants and animals – and of landscapes. Here, you'll find evergreen woodlands, savanna, and dune forests, lakes, lagoons, marshlands, papyrus swamps, reed beds, pans, floodplains, a sun-drenched coastline of great beauty and offshore waters noted for their coral reefs and their wealth of strikingly colourful marine creatures.

This diversity is the product of both history and geography. At one time, Maputaland lay beneath the ocean, which gradually receded to expose a flat, sandy plain where the last drainage channels left depressions, a series of shallow basins that gathered fresh water from the Pongola and other rivers to become the lakes and lakelets that are now such distinctive features of the region. Secondly, this is the meeting point of the tropical and subtropical zones, which accounts largely for its many and distinct ecosystems (five major ones in all) and its myriad habitats. The proclamation of the Greater St Lucia Wetland Park, which extends across some 260,000 hectares (1,100 square miles), has come none too soon: the region has been under mounting pressure from, among other things, mining and commercial interests, land developers and, not least of all, unregulated tourism. Happily, too, the park is now listed in terms of the Ramsar Convention as a wetland of international importance, and application has been made for its recognition as a World Heritage Site.

Lake and Reserve

Focus of the wetlands is Lake St Lucia, which covers 36,000 hectares (140 square miles), averages just a metre in depth and is really a system of lagoons that are connected to the sea by a narrow, 20-km-long channel. The waters are home to hippo (about 700 of them, found mostly in the south), crocodile and to a magnificent array of aquatic birds, notable among them the herons (fully 12 species are represented), great numbers of white pelicans, and a substantial population of breeding African fish eagles, supreme hunters of the African wetlands. The eastern banks are reed-grown and marshy; in the west they rise steeply to riverine forest. Among several attractive rivers and streams that feed the lake are the Mkuze and Hluhluwe, their waters helping maintain a constant balance between evaporation and the inflow of seawater.

Opposite: A giant sycamore fig, its roots submerged, spreads out across the water in the Mkuzi Game Reserve.

Top right: This hatching crocodile belongs to a clutch of up to 80 laid in a covered-in hollow near water. It will be well cared for by its parents, spending part of its infancy in the safety of a 'crèche'.

Above: Dense bush grows down to the water's edge at Charter's Creek.

Right: The flowers of the powder-puff tree form sprays that can be up to 60 centimetres (24 inches) in length.

Bottom left: The massive jaws of the Nile crocodile.

Bottom right: Hippos are normally placid enough, but territorial battles are savage, often fatal affairs.

Hippos are probably the noisiest and most visible occupants of the lake, emerging at night to wander along their beaten paths in search of good grazing. An adult male might weigh up to 1,800 kilograms (4,000 pounds) and is not to be trifled with: its curved, tusk-like teeth, set in massive jaws, can snap a crocodile (or a human) in two with a single bite. Visitors are warned to give these animals a wide berth, and to stay off known hippo paths after nightfall. At the other end of the size scale are the tiny prawns that are spawned at sea and drift into the lake, where they mature. Lake St Lucia, in fact, is South Africa's most important prawn habitat. It's also home to a myriad other crustaceans, and to a variety of fish – a magnet for discerning anglers.

The land around the estuary and a kilometre wide strip of reedbed, grassland and woodland around the lake are known as St Lucia Park, location of the Charter's Creek and Fanie's Island camps and camping sites. Here one can buy bait and hire a boat (not powered) and, from the Creek, embark on launch trips. The two-hour Isikhova and the slightly shorter Umkhumbe trails, both based on Charter's Creek, lead through the coastal forest and sections of the lake shore. Wildlife in the forests includes the nyala, duiker, reedbuck, porcupine, and vervet and samango monkey. Bushpig venture out at night. The village of St Lucia Estuary is the gateway to the lake's eastern shores, where the world's

loftiest vegetated dunes look down on wetlands and grasslands that support a host of often secretive animals and an attractively prolific bird life. The grasses sustain large numbers of reedbuck (this is said to be the highest concentration of the antelope in the world), buffalo, kudu, bushbuck and duiker.

The village boasts hotels, guesthouses, camping sites, shops, restaurants and the elegant lake cruiser *Santa Lucia*, which takes 80 passengers on comfortable 90-minute excursions three times a day. The Crocodile Centre, just to the north, provides a sharp insight into ways of these primeval creatures and of the role they play in the natural order. Here, too, you'll find interpretive displays on the whole of the St Lucia system.

To the south are stands of ancient forest of the coastal dune type. The trees are especially thick around Mapelane, where the Mfolozi River (which forms the park's southern boundary) reaches the sea, and include several wild fig species, red milkwood, ilala palm, tamboti, marula, podberry and black mangrove, all draped and entwined with creepers. Self-contained log cabins cater for overnighting visitors.

The flanking beaches, and especially the sands that stretch pristine and golden far to the north, play host to the annual influx of loggerheads and leatherbacks, giant, cumbersome, gentle and largely defenceless sea turtles that arrive from as far away as Kenyan waters, more than 2,000 kilometres (1,300 miles) distant, in order to breed along the Maputaland coast. They mate offshore, some time after which the females haul themselves onto the beach, at dusk, to deposit their precious eggs – up to 150 of them – in holes excavated with their powerful flippers. About ten weeks later the hatchlings begin their perilous journey to the sea, many of them falling victim to gulls and ghost crabs en route, and even more to the predators of the ocean.

Above: Trailists follow a dune ridge near Cape Vidal.

Bottom left: Grooming one another is an essential part of the vervet monkey's social pattern.

Bottom right: The long-legged serval, a medium-sized and mainly nocturnal cat, is agile enough to catch a bird in flight.

False Bay Park

The large, westerly bulge of the lake juts into a plateau of coastal bush known for its large game animals, among them nyala, suni and waterbuck, reedbuck, duiker, bush-pig and warthog, vervet and samango monkey and porcupine. Bird life is probably richer here than anywhere else in the park, and the arrival of the flamingo flocks – as many as 20,000 birds at a time, it's reckoned – is a sight that will live in the memory. Other species include the golden-tailed woodpecker, usually seen in pairs, noisily rapping against a dead tree-trunk; purple-crested louries hopping among the upper branches as they search for wild figs, their favourite food; the puffback shrike, descriptively known in Afrikaans as *sneeubal* (snowball), secretively exploring the upper branches, and the the African fish eagle, supreme hunter of the wetlands. Added attractions of the False Bay area are its pleasant picnic sites and the six-hour (eight-kilometre, or five-mile) open-ended Dugundlovu Trail, which is much favoured by birding enthusiasts. An optional deviation along the trail is a ten-kilometre (six-mile) circular route that takes in an attractive waterfall.

Mfabeni and Tewate

At the other side of the St Lucia estuary, occupying the central part of the narrow strip of land that separates lake from sea, are the rare dune forest and coastal grassland of the Mfabeni section, home to leopard (locally extinct until fairly recently), reedbuck and other animals. To the north, beyond Cape Vidal, lies Tewate Wilderness Area, (formerly known as the Cape Vidal State Forest), renowned for its reedbuck and for forested dunes that tower a full 120 metres (400 feet) above the sea. On their landward side are the marshy grasslands that form the edge of the lake. The generous dune vegetation provides shelter for, among others, bushbuck, duiker, bush-pig, vervet and the long-haired samango monkey. Of more interest, perhaps, are the black rhino, buffalo and kudu that have been reintroduced to the area. Tewate is also something of a paradise for bird-watchers.

Five-day, four-night guided wilderness trails, which start from the base camp on Lake Bhangazi, near Cape Vidal, are conducted between March and October. A team of donkeys, classic beasts of burden, carry the provisions and other baggage.

Sodwana Bay National Park

The small park lies within the St Lucia Marine Reserve (itself a part of the wider wetland park) well to the north of Cape Vidal, and is a popular holiday and weekend destination, its boundaries embracing tiny lakes, swamplands, dune forests, incomparable beaches and a three-kilometre (two-mile) strip of warm blue ocean. Most visitors come for the scuba diving and sea fishing (the background buzz of ski-boats is a constant refrain): the crystal-clear waters yield marvellous catches of blue and black marlin, sailfish, tuna, king mackerel, wahoo and the beautiful, metallic blue-green and gold dorado. Amenities include log cabins, numerous camp sites, a supermarket, fish-weighing points and some 200 freezer units. The beaches are also among the giant loggerhead turtle's favoured nesting grounds; nighttime 'turtle tours' are laid on during December and January.

Other popular pastimes include beach walks, guided environmental awareness trails (at weekends and during the holiday season), self-guided walks and the five-kilometre (three-mile) Ngoboseleni Trail that leads through dune forest to a small coastal lake.

Left: The red-clawed mangrove crab is found in the muddy waters of the region's estuaries.

Below left: The female loggerhead turtle travels far to mate in the offshore waters of the region and to give birth on its beaches.

Below: Sodwana Bay is famed for its beautiful, rock-fringed beaches. Offshore are the world's most southerly coral reefs.

Right: A traditional fisherman of Kosi Bay inspects his fish trap or 'kraal'.

Below: The painted reed frog – a tiny creature with a surprisingly loud call.

The Northern Lakes

Beyond Sodwana Bay, and separated from the sea by a narrow belt of towering forested dunes, lies Lake Sibaya, southern Africa's largest expanse of fresh water and home to crocodile, hippo and to a quite superb complement of aquatic birds. The area is rather isolated, hot, humid, pleasantly tranquil in its aspects and moods. The wood, reed and thatch huts of the Baya 'wilderness camp' are set close to the lakeshore; there are hides for bird-watchers; trail guides are available, and boats (each with a coxwain) can be hired.

Even farther north, nudging the Mozambique border, is Kosi Bay – which is somewhat misnamed as the 'bay' is, in reality, a sequence of four largish lakes linked to the ocean by a broad estuary that narrows to the Kosi mouth. The lakes and their surrounds are tropically attractive, an appealing compound of limpid blue water, marshland and mangrove swamp, raffia, wild date and ilala palm and, along the seaboard, high sand dune. Here, too, you'll find hippo, crocodile and a fine array of birds, among them palmnut vulture, night and whitebacked heron.

Kosi Bay is also a highly rewarding fishing ground, both for sporting anglers and the local villagers. The latter, who belong to the Tembe group, still harvest the waters in the manner of their forefathers, erecting timber-boomed 'kraals' to enclose the fish, which are then driven through funnel-type channels into smaller enclosures, where they are speared.

Mkuzi Game Reserve

To the northwest of Lake St Lucia, and linked to the wetlands by a corridor of land, is the 40,000-hectare (150 square-mile) Mkuzi reserve. For the most part the area comprises flattish terrain, its western parts bounded by the Lebombo mountains, its varied habitats (savanna grassland, riverine forest and wetlands) sustaining a remarkably diverse bird life. The reserve's 400-plus avian species include the great concourse of waterfowl that gathers, with the crocodiles and hippos, on and around the shallow reaches of Nsumo Pan, largest of several seasonal bodies of water within the reserve. The nearby sycamore fig forest, some of whose trees (Ficus gnaphalocarpa) have attained a height of more than 25 metres (60 feet), is thought to be the finest of its kind in Africa (it's certainly so regarded by the local, fig-relishing monkeys).

Elephant, formerly plentiful in the area, were reintroduced in 1996 to join the reserve's rhino (of both the black and white kinds), giraffe, kudu, nyala, wildebeest, impala and many smaller antelope species. Also present are the elusive leopard and the swift, superbly streamlined cheetah.

Visitors can see much of this from the hides that have been erected around the various pans, and from strategically sited picnic spots. A network of game-viewing roads criss-crosses the flattish terrain (which enables one to enjoy wide views of the landscape and its animals), and there's a 77-kilometre (48-mile) auto trail that focuses on the Mkuzi reserve's ecology in general and its trees in particular.

Guided game walks set out each day; the three-kilometre Fig Forest Trail starts and ends at the car park at Nsumo Pan and, for the more energetic, there are a variety of guided wilderness trails (by prior arrangement).

Getting Around

Each of the reserves within the Greater St Lucia Wetland Park has its own system of walks and trails. The self-guided walks are clearly marked, and all are rewarding, especially for bird-watchers. Outstanding among these are Mkuzi's Fig Forest Trail, the Umvubu Trail in the Mfabeni section, and the Mziki Trail and its variations in the Tewate Wilderness Area. The KwaZulu-Natal Nature

Conservation Service produces useful brochures containing the latest information for visitors taking to the trails. Canoeing and powerboating are allowed on designated areas of the lake; the 80-seat cruiser *Santa Lucia*, complete with cocktail bar, tours the southern segment of the lake in style.

Staying There

Private accommodation is available in and around the village of St Lucia Estuary. The KwaZulu-Natal Nature Conservation Service operates five hutted camps and several caravan and camping sites within the area, namely at Sodwana Bay (eight-bed log cabins, 'de luxe' camping sites and a large, open main camp for tents and caravans); in the Tewate Wilderness Area (log cabins at Cape Vidal, north of St Lucia Estuary); at Charter's Creek and Fanie's Island, on the western shore of the lake; and in False Bay Park, where amenities are limited to a small, basic, rustic camp at Dugundlovu and about 20 shady and well-planned caravan and camping sites that overlook the lake.

Lake Sibaya has its Baya 'wilderness camp' and, on the seaboard close to the eastern shore of the lake, the Mabibi coastal camp site. The Kosi Bay Nature Reserve embraces three furnished (and most attractive) lodges, built from local materials and set on the Nhlange lakeshore, together with a number of camp sites.

Mkuzi's Nhlonhlela bush lodge is a cluster of well appointed two-bed reed-and-thatch huts set beside the lovely Nhlonhlela Pan, two tented bush camps (en suite facilities), a hutted camp and a caravan and camping site.

Above: Plains zebra drink their fill from the Mkuzi reserve's Nsumo Pan.

Above: One of the myriad species of moth found in and around the St Lucia wetlands.

Left: The stately giraffe, tall enough to reach the tender shoots of the topmost branches.

ITALA GAME RESERVE

A Sanctuary Reborn

Deep green valleys, hilly grasslands and dramatic ridges are among the distinguishing components of the Itala reserve, a scenically superb wilderness area tucked away in the valley of the Pongola River in northern KwaZulu-Natal.

Pongola – which means 'like a trough' and refers to the river's great length and the lack of easy crossings – is one of the most important of South Africa's perennial watercourses, running close to the boundary between the KwaZulu-Natal and Mpumalanga provinces and eventually flowing into Delagoa Bay, on the Mozambique coast, as the Maputa River. Its tributaries have carved their way down from the highveld plateau in the west, following steep-sided, grassy, sometimes wooded valleys that, in season, are ablaze with crimson aloes. Along their courses are delightful pools and rapids and stretches of riverine forest. The less rugged areas are covered with mixed savanna woodland and low-growing and light-crowned trees with, in many places, bushes that form a shrubby under-storey – ideal country for viewing, and photographing, wildlife.

Opposite: The white or square-lipped rhinoceros is the largest living land mammal after the elephant. Unlike its smaller black or hook-lipped cousin, it is primarily a grazer rather than a browser.

Top right: A trio of toadstools flourishes on a rhino midden in the Itala reserve.

Animals of the Park

Itala began life in 1972. The region had once accommodated the old Pongolo reserve, one of Africa's earliest conservation areas, but the project had long been abandoned and many, indeed most, of the animals had become locally extinct: only a few of the larger life forms, notably the crocodile and the solitary, secretive leopard, had survived the years of neglect and human predation, so the conservationists had to start more or less from scratch.

The restocking exercise has been a stunning success. Species that were brought in and are now flourishing are elephant, white and black rhino, buffalo, giraffe, zebra, blue wildebeest, tsessebe, kudu, impala, red hartebeest and, in the hillier parts, the agile and sure-footed klipspringer. Among the reintroduced predators is the brown hyaena.

One of the more distinctive of Itala's herbivores is the blue wildebeest, distinguished from its black cousin not, primarily, by its colour (greyish-brown as opposed to a dark brown) but by its prominent, erect mane and a long tail that almost sweeps the ground. The blue is also the larger and heavier of the two, and has humped shoulders and a distinctly sloping back – a physique that accounts for the animal's unusual 'rocking horse' motion when covering the ground at a gallop. The blue wildebeest is notoriously inquisitive, and will often stand still and stare at an intruder before suddenly whirling about and galloping away.

Location: Itala is situated in northern KwaZulu-Natal, close to Vryheid and close to Louwsburg.

Climate: Summers tend to be very hot; winter days mild, the nights sometimes freezing.

When to go: The reserve is open daily from sunrise to sunset. June to October are the best game-viewing months.

Getting there: The entrance is reached through the village of Louwsburg, off the R69 between Vryheid and Magudu. The reserve's tarred airstrip can take most types of private aircraft.

Facilities: Restaurant, curio shop and mini-supermarket, swimming pool, conference centre, airstrip. Guided walks; conducted day- and night-game drives are especially geared to fly-in safaris.

Wildlife: Abundant: Itala is home to more than 70 mammal and over 300 bird species.

Landscapes: These are spectacular in parts: the land falls steeply from the highveld plateau in the south to the basin of the Pongola River (a drop of almost 1,000 m or 3,250 feet). The rugged cliffs tower over a countryside of acacia thornveld, woodland, savanna and hilly grassland, the wrinkled appearance of the slopes betraying signs of ancient weathering. Many of the game-viewing roads lead to scenically superb viewsites.

Permits and reservations: Accommodation must be reserved in advance through the KwaZulu-Natal Nature Conservation Service (see page 174). Guided walks: book at the reserve's office on the preceding day. Day visitors obtain entry permits at the gate.

Precautions: Ticks can sometimes be troublesome.

Itala's Birds

The varied nature of the land and its flora create habitats for a fine array of birds – about 320 species in all, among which are the martial and the black eagles and Wahlberg's eagle, which usually nests in trees. Itala is also home to the black-breasted snake-eagle, the commonly seen African hawk eagle and the African fish eagle, arguably Africa's most spectacular avian hunter. The bald ibis, a threatened species with a fleeting resemblance to the domesticated turkey, maintains a thriving breeding colony within the park. These attractive, glossy dark-green birds, found in groups of up to 20, wander across the veld probing for insects and other small delicacies with their long, slender red bills.

Getting Around

Itala's network of gravel-surfaced roads, which are negotiable by an ordinary family car, provides fine game viewing both from the vehicle and at the attractive picnic sites and observation points en route: the open nature of much of the countryside enables the visitor to see far more clearly, and for greater distances, than in reserves such as Hluhluwe-Umfolozi (see page 28) and Mkuzi (page 44). For the more energetic, there are day walks, each accompanied by a guide or field ranger (a reminder that the animals, however 'tame' they might seem, are wild and can be dangerous). The length, duration and itinerary of these outings varies, depending on the character and preferences of the group.

Staying There

Ntshondwe Camp is magnificently set under the weathered cliffs of the high escarpment in the western section of the reserve. Despite its size (it can host more than 200 guests) it blends beautifully with the rugged background. It also offers superb vistas of the bush-covered valley below, and its waterhole, flanked by walkways and hides, is well patronized by game animals and birds. Accommodation comprises two-, four- and six-bed chalets (most self-catering, all of them serviced) and a six-

Top: The bald ibis spends much of its day walking the veld, probing for insects and small animals.

Above: Redthorn, like many other acacias, puts out masses of fluffy, ball-like flowers from springtime to mid-summer.

Right: The giraffe is the world's tallest animal, reaching a height of around five metres (16 feet). It can gallop at speeds of more than 50 km/h (31 mph).

bed lodge complete with resident chef. There's also a fully licensed restaurant, a takeaway service and a cocktail bar. The nearby, luxurious conference centre, virtually a self-contained village, comprises an auditorium, two smaller venues and two dozen or so chalets.

Sited away from the main tourist routes are Thalu, Mbizo and Mhlanageni, three small, delightful bush camps. Each has its own caretaker and field ranger (who will take you out on walks) and its own boma or enclosure. All have lovely views.

Above: Itala's Ntshondwe Camp is set on a plateau sheltered by the hills and cliffs that make up much of the reserve's landscape.

Left: Although the eland, Africa's largest antelope, is principally a browser, it sometimes uses its fore-hooves to dig for tubers, roots and melons.

THE DRAKENSBERG AND FOOTHILLS

The Eastern Rampart

Location: The park occupies the mountainous strip running along KwaZulu-Natal's eastern border.

Climate: Summers can be hot and fairly humid, most rain falling between December and February. Winters are mild to cold, the peaks often covered in snow.

When to go: Each season has its splendour; the park remains open throughout the year.

Getting there: The 'Berg and Little 'Berg areas are accessible from the N3, the main Johannesburg–Durban highway. Exits are well signposted.

Facilities: Walks and trails; Bushman (San) art site museums; bird hides; picnic sites; accommodation and basic shops at some camps; horses, tack and trout-fishing tackle for hire; hotels and lodges outside the reserve areas.

Activities: Walking, hiking, climbing, camping, trout-fishing, studying rock art, birds, plants.

Wildlife: The Drakensberg and its rugged foothills are renowned for their bird life (most notably the raptors). Most reserves are home to antelope species and to other smaller mammals.

Landscapes: High mountains, deep ravines, and a fantasia of cliff, buttress, dragon-toothed ridge, cave, ledge and balancing rock; upland streams, grasslands, dense forest patches. The vistas are sensational.

Permits and reservations: Day visitors to protected areas obtain entry and fishing permits on admission. Accommodation within them needs to be booked well in advance, through the KwaZulu-Natal Nature Conservation Service (see page 174).

Precautions: Treat the mountains with respect at all times; never climb alone; if possible, take an experienced guide.

The Drakensberg is a scenically grand, in parts awe-inspiring mountain range that extends for more than a thousand kilometres, from the Eastern Cape through KwaZulu-Natal and Mpumalanga to the Northern Province. The entire range and, especially, the towering segment known as the KwaZulu-Natal Drakensberg, exerts a profound influence on weather patterns: this is one of the very few southern African regions where annual rains exceed the 1,400-millimetre (55-inch) mark, the run-off augmented by the melting of the winter snows. In fact the country's most important perennial rivers rise in or near the Drakensberg, among them the Orange, Vaal, Tugela, Pongolo, Usutu and Letaba.

Of all its sections, that within KwaZulu-Natal offers the most formidable obstacle to transport, to the encroachment of man – and it is here that the natural landscape has been best preserved. Reserves and wilderness areas adjoin one another in an almost unbroken line, most of them components of the wider Drakensberg Park. Thabantshonyana, at

3,482 metres (11,421 feet, and just across the border in Lesotho), is the highest peak but others such as Giant's Castle, Cathedral Peak, Cathkin Peak, Champagne Castle and Mont-aux-Sources, are perhaps better known: they are the most prominent features of the huge tract of protected countryside running along the Lesotho border from Mont-aux-Sources southwards. Visitors come from afar to challenge the heights, to explore on foot and on horseback, to savour the vistas and the clean, clear mountain air, to enjoy the snows of the higher slopes, the crystal streams and the sheer spaciousness of this rare and lovely land.

Life in the Mountains

The Drakensberg Park is noted principally for its splendid landscapes, its birds and its flora, but it also has its animals. Eland, bushbuck, grey rhebok, mountain reedbuck and the impressively agile klipspringer are among the larger mammals; baboon, porcupine and rock dassie (or hyrax) can also be seen. The bird lists are impressive – more than 140 species have been recorded in the Giant's Castle and 185 in the Royal Natal sanctuaries. Among the larger birds is the bearded vulture or lammergeier (*Gypaetus barbatus*), its wedge-shaped tail and dark beard immediate aids to

Map labels:
R516
Royal Natal National Park
Mont-aux-Sources
3282 m
R74
Bergville
Woodstock Dam
Lesotho
Winterton
R600
R74
Cathedral Peak 3004 m
Cathedral Peak
Frere
to Durban
N3
Monk's Cowl
Central 'Berg Resorts
N
Ntabamhlope
Giant's Castle
Durban
Kamberg Nature Reserve
Loteni Nature Reserve
Mkhomazi Wilderness Area
Sani Pass
Mzimkulwana Nature Reserve
Mzimkulu Wilderness Area
Mzimkulwana Nature Reserve
Underberg
R617
Lesotho

Opposite, top: The soaring heights of the Drakensberg.

Opposite, bottom: The Amphitheatre viewed face-on; in the foreground are the upper reaches of the Tugela River.

Top right: A multi-hued grasshopper of the uplands.

identification as it soars from its untidy nest on some inaccessible shelf high up on a cliff face. The bearded vulture, a rare species, is known for the way it breaks the bones of carrion into digestible pieces: it finds a large, flattish rock, soars high in the air with an obstinate bone held in its hooked beak and then, when precisely over the target, it lets go, quickly descending to enjoy the shattered fragments. These sites, or ossuaries, are a sure indicator of the bird's presence. Another stately raptor is the black eagle (*Aquila verreauxii*), known for its regal soaring and gliding, and for its thunderbolt dives on the birds and small mammals it feeds on. Although it occurs more widely than the bearded vulture, the black eagle's numbers are also declining.

Plant life is more varied than most visitors expect: the mountains and their foothills sustain some 2,200 species, of which about 83 are orchids. Trout have been introduced to most rivers in the area, which has become something of a mecca for discerning anglers.

Royal Natal National Park

The 7,400-hectare (29-square mile) park, which received its regal prefix when Britain's royal family visited the area in 1947, is renowned for its magnificent landscapes, which include the huge, curving rock face of The Amphitheatre and the long leap (some 853 metres, or 2,800 feet in total) of the Tugela Falls, the world's second highest waterfall. The Tugela River, which flows eastwards to the Indian Ocean, rises on the Mont-aux-Sources ('mountain of springs'), its gorge graced by extensive stands of stately yellowwood trees.

A scenic road runs along the edge of the river's upper reaches for part of its course, and no fewer than 31 hikes and foot trails have been mapped out, ranging from the gentle Otto's Walk to the 45-kilometre (28-mile) Mont-aux-Sources route. A slightly less orthodox but most appealing way to explore Royal Natal is on horseback: bridle paths have been laid out, and horses and tack can be hired at the adjacent Rugged Glen Nature Reserve. Tendele Camp offers chalets, bungalows, a lodge and cottages. The park also encloses a large, privately run hotel (scheduled for replacement by a 200-bedroom rest camp), and there are camping sites at tree-shaded Mahai and at Rugged Glen, close to the park entrance.

Giant's Castle

Until fairly recent times – till about the mid-19th century – the 43,000-hectare (166-square mile) Giant's Castle area was home to clans of Bushmen (or San), whose rock

paintings remain a poignant reminder of these 'beautiful people', perhaps the greatest of all prehistoric artists, and their long occupation. The caves and overhangs serve as 'galleries' for an enormous profusion of paintings. Indeed, fully 40 per cent of the Bushman's artistic gift to southern Africa is to be found in the KwaZulu-Natal Drakensberg. Decorated caves offer visitors a sharp insight into the culture and its visual legacy. Often depicted in the paintings is the eland, a large and gentle antelope that still flourishes here, along with reedbuck, oribi, blesbok, hartebeest and rhebok. Bird life is especially impressive; among the 140 or so species recorded are bearded vulture, waterbirds such as egret and stork, and the blue crane, which seems to favour the pools along Oribi Ridge. Here, too, there is a vulture hide. A special attraction along some of the longer guided wilderness hikes are the nights one spends in the cosy recesses of a sandstone cave. There are also shorter, self-guided walks. Accommodation at Giant's Castle is varied, embracing cottages, bungalows, a lodge, and secluded mountain huts.

Kamberg Nature Reserve

What is known as the Little Berg (the foothills zone) is the setting for this smallish (7,200-hectare, or 28-square mile) but immensely attractive sanctuary, haven for a fascinating variety of floral species and for antelope, and the site of a trout hatchery that supplies many of KwaZulu-Natal's streams. Appropriately, trout fishing, in river and dam, is a popular pastime among Kamberg's visitors. Well-routed walks lead among the hills and by the banks of the Mooi River, through indigenous vegetation that includes protea-veld, yellowwoods and tree ferns (of which five species occur in South Africa). Large mammals include the black wildebeest (KwaZulu-Natal's heraldic animal), oribi, duiker, eland, hartebeest, grey rhebok and reedbuck. Again, there are some fine examples of rock art to be seen. The Mooi River Trail has a four-kilometre (three-mile) main section with several optional loops, and has been planned with the physically disabled in mind. Accommodation comprises a small hutted camp, a self-catering five-bed chalet and a spacious old farmhouse (for groups of up to ten).

Above: The newly born, ribbon-like Tugela plunges over the Amphitheatre's rim in an 850-metre (2,800-foot) series of sparkling cascades.

Opposite, top: The Cape clawless otter, one of the largest of its family, can sometimes be seen on and near the river banks.

Opposite, centre: One of the Drakensberg's more elusive animals is the caracal, a medium-sized cat famed for its amazing agility.

Opposite, bottom: The spotted-necked otter, smaller than its clawless cousin.

Right: The infant Tugela River plunges through its magical gorge.

Bottom left: Cape weavers are an attractive component of the Drakensberg's prolific bird life.

Bottom centre: The mountains sustain more than 800 species of flowering plant, including a splendid variety of lilies.

Bottom right: The red bishop, one of the Drakensberg's more colourful birds.

Opposite: The Giant's Castle Reserve is renowned for its scenic splendour, its birds of prey and its Bushman paintings.

Loteni Nature Reserve

This Little Berg area encloses the dramatically scenic valley of the Loteni River, a tributary of the Mkomazi and well stocked with brown trout. The name Loteni ('ashes') refers to the burnt appearance of the dark shale exposed in cuttings where the river flows among the bush- and grass-covered hills. Reedbuck, grey rhebok, eland, oribi and duiker graze on the slopes; bird life includes the Cape vulture and the black stork, a visiting migrant during the European winter. Storks are frequently seen among antelope, stalking the grasslands in search of the large insects, frogs, mice and small reptiles that comprise their diet. Several trails lead away from Loteni camp site, including the 12-kilometre (7½ mile) Eagle route, along which there are superb views. Other easier paths bring you to Ash Cave, on the Loteni River, and to Yellowwood Cave. An overnight route (take your own tent) leads via Buttress Pass to Redi Peak, which rises to 3,341 metres (10,958 feet) above sea level. Loteni has a hutted camp of self-contained bungalows, and a camping site.

Southern Drakensberg

Sprawling to the south are the huge, pristine, lonely Mkhomazi and Mzimkulu wildernesses, areas that are rich in their flora, beautiful in their setting of high mountain, grasslands and deep green forests, and remarkable in their array of birds of prey, among them black eagle, martial eagle, jackal buzzard and bearded vulture. Cutting through these southern sanctuaries is a dusty road that leads you up, through a series of dizzy hairpin bends and switchbacks, to the soaring Sani Pass, the only direct road link between KwaZulu-Natal and Lesotho. The pass rises to 2,377 metres (7,787 feet) above sea level, and you'll need a 4x4 to negotiate the route – but the journey is well worth the effort: the mountain-and-valley vistas are memorable.

Staying There

Visitors have a wide choice of accommodation beyond the camps within the reserve areas. Especially popular are the so-called 'resort hotels' scattered around the foothills, some luxurious, many of them old-established, unpretentious, friendly and supremely comfortable places catering for the more casual vacationer.

GOLDEN GATE HIGHLANDS NATIONAL PARK

The Gilded Uplands of the Eastern Free State

This splendid expanse of countryside, set in the valley of the Little Caledon River in the northeastern Free State, is well named for here, beneath the grandeur of the high Maluti mountains, sandstone and iron oxides have combined to create a quite remarkable fantasia of warm, earthy colours.

Just as compelling is the ruggedness of the terrain. Over the aeons rain and wind have sculpted the sandstone peaks, ridges, steep cliffs and buttresses into stark and often bizarre shapes, their dramatic outlines enhanced by the reds and ochres, the oranges, yellows and golden browns in which they are painted. The 'gate' itself refers to a massive twin buttress known as the Brandwag (Sentinel); among many other notable formations are the distinctive, and descriptive, Mushroom Rocks. The geological type is known as Clarens sandstone, named after the pretty little village nearby which, in turn, commemorates the Swiss town in which erstwhile Transvaal president Paul Kruger died in exile (in 1904). The area's many caves and deep shelters are a reminder that this natural building material was, at one time, called 'cave sandstone'.

Opposite: Streams from the catchment area of Golden Gate feed the Little Caledon River and sculpt the exposed, variously coloured sandstones of the area.

Top right: The rare bearded vulture is a bird of the mountains, often seen gliding at speed along the high ridges.

The Caledon's banks are beautifully embowered with willow trees; the veld graced, at times, by arum lilies, watsonias, red hot pokers and fire lilies. For the most part visitors come to enjoy the landscapes, their flora and the invigorating mountain air, although the 12 000-hectare (46-square mile) park is also haven to a fair number of animals. Among the larger mammals you'll see are wildebeest, Burchell's zebra, eland, blesbok, oribi and springbok, all of which have been reintroduced to the area. Birds include the bald ibis and the rare bearded vulture (or lamergeier), both of which breed high on the cliffs; the majestic black eagle; the blue crane (South Africa's national bird), the jackal buzzard and the secretarybird.

Getting Around

A well-maintained road cuts through the park. Nature trails of up to five hours enable you to combine game-viewing with a pleasant scenic outing. One does not have to book for these, but the longer (two-day) Rhebok Hiking Trail does require an advance reservation. Guided excursions and night drives can be arranged. Horse riding is also an option; mounts may be hired near the park's western entrance.

Staying There

Accommodation includes hotel suites, rooms and cottages at Brandwag Rest Camp; bungalows, camping and caravan sites at Glen Reenen. Wilgenhof Hostel, used for youth groups, houses 80 people in four dormitories. Nearby Clarens, and Bethlehem just to the north, offer hotels and guesthouses.

Location: The park lies 58 km (36 miles) southeast of Bethlehem in the northeastern Free State.

Climate: Highveld summers are pleasantly warm (though nights can be distinctly chilly), and sometimes noisy with thundershowers. Winters are cold, the higher slopes often mantled in snow.

When to go: The park, which is bisected by a public road (the east-west R712), is open all year round.

Getting there: From the west, take the R26 through Ficksburg, followed by the R712. From Harrismith, in the east, take either the R712 or the N5 to Kestell and then follow the untarred but highly scenic route directly to the park. The shortest route from Bethlehem, in the north, is via the R712.

Facilities: Shops, restaurant, picnic sites; natural swimming pool at Glen Reenan; hikes, walks, horse riding, network of game-viewing roads; bowling green, tennis courts, nine-hole golf course. Among the area's showpieces is the fascinating Basuto cultural village.

Landscapes: Rugged, multi-hued Clarens sandstone formations; an infinite subtlety of light and shade; grand mountain backdrop. Caves and pockets of indigenous forest invite exploration.

Wildlife: The park is known mainly for its scenery, but is also home to black wildebeest, Burchell's zebra, oribi, eland, springbok and blesbok. Bird life fairly prolific: the 160 or so recorded species include black eagle, bearded vulture and bald ibis.

Permits and reservations: Day visitors obtain permits on admission; reservations are not required for the shorter walks. Accommodation, and a place on the Rhebok Trail, are booked through the South African National Parks (see page 174).

THE WILD COAST

Land of Many Rivers

Transkei, homeland of the Xhosa people, an 'independent' state during the apartheid years and now embraced by the Eastern Cape province, ranks among the most exquisite parts of southern Africa's extensive coastal belt.

The region stretches from the Great Kei River northeastwards to the Mtamvuna, a 250-kilometre (155-mile) stretch of sand-fringed bays, lagoons and estuaries, rugged cliffs and rocky reefs that probe dangerously out to sea, and of a score and more attractive holiday resorts and villages, most of them clustered around the river-mouths. Of the latter, there are many: fully 18 substantial watercourses flow down from the rolling hills of the hinterland, all but one slicing their way through rock and soil to discharge into the ocean in conventional fashion. The exception is the Mfihlelo, which strikes a stratum of harder rock and tumbles directly into the sea from high up on Waterfall Bluff.

Unusual, too, is the Mpako River, which reaches the sea via a tunnel that it has worn through a rock-

face that now, as a massive detached cliff, lies far out in the surf and is known as the Hole in the Wall. Its flat top, big enough to accommodate several football fields, is still mantled in greenery; the Indian Ocean rollers thunder their way through the arched opening below. The local people call the cliff *esiKhaleni*, or 'the place of noise'.

Idyllic though the seascapes seem, ocean and shoreline can be menacing in their moods. Over the centuries they have claimed a great many ships, their wrecks – a few of them visible, most hidden by the drifting sands of the seabed – testifying to the ferocity of the storms that sometimes lash these shores, and to the treachery of the currents and jagged reefs.

Six Sanctuaries

Transkei is rural country but densely populated, and over the decades the land, the coastal forests and marine resources have been over-exploited. But recently reinforced conservation measures hold promise for the future, and the coastal strip remains a picture of rare and haunting beauty – especially in the protected areas.

The Umtamvuna Nature Reserve, in the far northeast, lies along the south bank of the Mtamvuna River, whose tall riverine forest serves as home to baboon and monkey, to a number of antelope species, including oribi, and to the secretive leopard. The African fish eagle

Opposite: The Wild Coast is so called for its sudden storms, but for much of the time it wears a tranquil face.

Top right: The shell of the abalone, or *perlemoen*. These shellfish are a prized table delicacy the world over.

Location: The southeastern coast of the Eastern Cape.

Climate: Winters are mild with occasional cold spells; summer days can be very hot. Most of the rain falls in summer.

When to go: Spring and autumn are the dry months and are usually pleasantly warm. The gates of the reserves are open from sunrise to sunset throughout the year.

Getting there: The road between Umtata and Port St Johns (R61) is tarred. Port St Johns is also accessible from the N2, via Flagstaff and Lusikisiki. Access to Dwesa and Cwebe is by gravel road from Idutywa or Viedgeville; a fairly good tarred road leads from Viedgeville to Coffee Bay. Mkambathi is reached by gravel roads from Lusikisiki, Flagstaff and Bizana.

Facilities: Self-guided walks and trails; coastal and resort centres offer a range of facilities; the seaboard has several lodges and hotels, most prominent of which is the Wild Coast Sun complex.

Activities: Walks; hikes; watersports; scuba diving and snorkling; anglers are well rewarded; wide range of leisure activities, including golf, at the Wild Coast Sun.

Wildlife: Bird life is abundant; antelope species have been successfully reintroduced to the reserves.

Landscapes: The rugged coastal strip embraces forest, grassland, rock and imposing cliff formations.

Permits and reservations: Permits for day visits to the reserves are obtainable on arrival; accommodation must be reserved in advance.

Precautions: Beware of sharks in estuaries; never cross river mouths on an outgoing tide. The general area has faced something of a security problem; don't drive or walk through the countryside on your own.

Above: The Hole in the Wall, a massive detached cliff eroded by the pounding of the breakers, is the Wild Coast's most striking physical feature.

Below: Their isolation and long robes identify these young Xhosa men as members of an initiation school.

and the rare, endangered Cape vulture are among the 80 or so species recorded on the local bird list. Down the coast is Mkambathi Nature Reserve, a microcosm of the Wild Coast with its long, lonely beaches and wide estuaries that, inland, narrow to waterfalls cascading through steep, forested gorges. The rare Pondoland palm or *mkambathi*, also known as the Pondo coconut, grows only along the Mtentu and Msikaba rivers; its fruit resembles a tiny coconut, and miniature trees are easily propagated from the seed. Bird life is prolific (the forest species especially so), and the grasslands sustain zebra, eland, wildebeest, red hartebeest and blesbok. The

Msikaba River, which is 33 metres (110 feet) wide in places, forms a broad, shallow estuary on a sandy beach widely noted for the variety and often exquiste beauty of its myriad seashells.

The Silaka Nature Reserve, just south of the little resort town of Port St Johns, is a pleasant mixture of rugged coast, evergreen forest and grassland. Its many shoreline rock pools invite exploration and Bird Island, heavily colonized by white-breasted cormorants, is within easy splashing depth. Tall trees line the banks of the Gxwaleni River which, here and there, forms quiet pools thick with water lilies. Among forest birds is the shy and colourful Knysna lourie.

Hluleka Nature Reserve, some 30 kilometres (20 miles) from Port St Johns, is also noted for the bird life of its plains and forests, while its rocky seaboard is a favourite haunt of anglers. Footpaths criss-cross much of the area, offering a choice of game-viewing walks and a chance to see the spectacular African fish eagle, Cape parrot, Knysna lourie, osprey, ground hornbill and the rare green coucal, which is notable for its conspicuous yellow bill. Also seen and heard is Burchell's coucal, popularly known as the rainbird, whose beautiful, bubbling song is said to herald rainy weather. Hluleka is known for the myriad, colourful butterflies that decorate the countryside in spring and summer.

Farther down the seaboard are the adjoining Dwesa and Cwebe reserves, established about a century ago as forest sanctuaries, havens for creeper-garlanded

stinkwood, Cape ebony and yellowwood. The two areas are bisected by the Mbashe River, which discharges into the sea through Africa's most southerly mangrove swamps. Mangroves are trees and shrubs adapted to the saline conditions of the inter-tidal zones of estuaries and placid shores, and only a few species occur beyond the tropics. Here you'll find the rare mangrove kingfisher and the lovely Narina trogon. Present, too, are a few crocodile; game, which may sometimes be seen on the beach, includes buffalo, eland, blesbok, warthog and several species of small antelope.

Getting Around

Running inland and parallel to the coast is the main highway (N2), off which lesser roads, ranging from the good to the indifferent, wind their way through and over the hills to the shoreline. River-canoeing is a slightly unusual but marvelouslly restful way of seeing landscapes and wildlife that might otherwise be missed. Canoes may be hired at Mkambathi.

Above: The water mongoose forages in search of small rodents and insects. It also takes frogs, crabs and shellfish.

Right: The bluff cliffs at Morgan Bay provide shelter for a bathing beach and tranquil lagoon.

Above: A myriad seashells, cast up by the warm waters of the Indian Ocean, adorn the beaches of the area.

Right: Trailing plants, able to resist both wind and the saline environment, bind the sandy stretches near Bashee Point.

The 280-kilometre (175-mile), 25-day, open-ended Wild Coast Trail, divided into five variable sections, begins in the north and offers both a fine sense of adventure and close encounters with the animals, birds, plants and marine life of this lovely coastal strip. Features of special interest en route include the Hole in the Wall, Brazen Head, and the enchanting Cathedral Rock. There's good angling along the coast, but remember that you may not gather bait within a nature reserve. Basic camps have been established at intervals.

Staying There

Rest camps at Dwesa-Cwebe (in the Cwebe section), Hluleka and Mkambathi offer self-contained chalets. One can buy firewood in the reserves, but very little else, so bring your own provisions. Camping is not permitted in the proclaimed areas. Conventional accommodation – comfortable resort hotels which offer the standard amenities, or bed-and-breakfast establishments – is available at Qolora Mouth, Mazeppa Bay, Coffee Bay, Umngazi Mouth and Port St Johns.

Right: The wreck of the *Jacaranda*, which came to grief in 1971, is just one of scores of ships that have foundered in the treacherous waters of the Wild Coast over the centuries.

ADDO ELEPHANT NATIONAL PARK

A Place that was once a 'Hunter's Hell'

It was the dense valley bushveld of the Addo, impenetrable to man, that saved the great elephant herds of the Cape from total extinction some 80 years ago.

During the decades before then the elephants had caused havoc in the cultivated lands of the region and, finally, although the animals had been greatly reduced in number, the farmers hired professional hunters to exterminate the last of them. Just 15 out of a total of 135 survived the slaughter, eleven of whom fled into the dense spekboom bush of an area that was once described as 'a hunter's hell'. There they were protected by the terrain, and by outraged public opinion – and there they remain.

The park, a pristine expanse of valley, mountain-slope and plain situated not far from Port Elizabeth – the Eastern Cape's industrial hub – is an ideal refuge for many forms of wildlife. The bush, rarely higher than 3.5 metres (11½ feet), comprises a thorny tangle of acacia, boerboon, bush guarri and spekboom (also known as 'elephant's food') – all of which looks somewhat unappetizing to the human eye, but the vegetation in fact has high nutritive value. So much so, indeed, that the land's carrying capacity for elephant (2.7 animals per hectare) is four times greater than that of any other similar-sized area in Africa. Taller trees grow on the slopes and in some of the ravines; shorter plants include many types of shrub and succulent.

Top right: An Addo elephant. Like its kind elsewhere, it likes to smear itself with mud as protection against both the sun and stinging insects.

The herd, now more than 280 strong, roams an enclosed area of some 12,000 hectares (45 square miles) and, although one would expect its members to be shy, inheriting a collective memory of man as an agent of death, they are thoroughly familiar with the sight, smell and sound of vehicles and surprisingly relaxed in the presence of visitors.

They are not, as was once thought, genetically different from the African elephant, although there are local variations – the tusks, for instance, are usually carried by the males only, and tend to be rather on the small side.

There is little naturally occurring surface water in the park, so artificial waterholes (boreholes) have been built to sustain the wildlife, and to create excellent viewing areas. In the early years the elephants were coaxed from the bush with citrus fruit – to which they became addicted. The practice provoked aggression and was eventually stopped, but it left its legacy: today, no visitors may take citrus into the park, not even for their own consumption.

The old-time hunters wiped out many of the region's animals, but a good number of the original wildlife species are being reintroduced, gradually, and the park's residents now include the endangered black rhino, African buffalo (which were rezoned along with the elephants), kudu, eland and smaller antelope, warthog and several the smaller carnivores such as jackal and caracal. More then 180 bird species have been recorded.

To the northwest of the elephant area is the park's hilly, scenically splendid Zuurberg section, notable for its varied and attractive vegetation. This includes the rare

Location: About 80 km (50 miles) northeast of Port Elizabeth in the Eastern Cape Province.

Climate: Rain falls throughout the year, but mostly in summer. Summer days are hot to warm; winter days can be chilly, the nights cold, but frost free.

When to go: Gates are open from 7 am to 7 pm daily. Midsummer is the busiest time; the elephants are at their most active early in the morning on warm days, though they also gather at waterholes during the hottest hours.

Getting there: Take the N2 highway and break off along the R335 for Addo about 10 km (6 miles) northwest of Port Elizabeth. When travelling from Grahamstown, turn right from the N2 onto the N10 and, 5 km (3½ miles) on, turn left for Addo.

Facilities: Restaurant serving á la carte meals, shop (basic provisions), bird hide (beside a dam, near camp) and game hide (at waterhole); picnic and barbecue sites (with ablutions), swimming pool for resident visitors; game watching from your own vehicle; guided night drives; bird and game observation hides.

Wildlife: The elephants are the main attraction, but also in residence are black rhino, buffalo and many antelope; small carnivores, and a bird list of some 185 species.

Permits and reservations: Permits for day visitors are obtainable on entry, and are also required by visitors intent on embarking on the Zuurberg walks or the Spekboom Trail. Accommodation should be booked through the South African National Parks (see page 174) a good 12 months in advance.

Precautions: No citrus fruits of any type may be taken into the park.

Above: A breeding herd of elephant seen against a background of the dense, nutritious 'Addo bush' on which the animals thrive.

Right: Red hartebeest ewe and calf. Females usually leave the herd to give birth in a secluded place.

Zuurberg cushion bush and the Zuurberg cycad, neither of which occurs elsewhere. In some of the shadier ravines, evergreen forest survives in small pockets. Here, too, animals are being reintroduced; numbered among the established wildlife population are bushbuck, mountain reedbuck, grey rhebok, blue duiker and the once endangered Cape mountain zebra.

Getting Around, Staying There

Addo incorporates 43 kilometres (27 miles) of well maintained and clearly signposted game-viewing roads; night drives can be arranged. Some of the routes, however, are closed after heavy rains.

Two walks, of one and four hours' duration respectively, start and finish near the entrance to the Zuurberg section. The six-kilometre (3½-mile) Spekboom Trail winds its way through a botanical reserve (which is

Far left: The flightless ostrich, largest of the world's birds, features among the Addo's wildlife.

Left: Suricates, or meerkats, stand upright for a better view – and to warm themselves in the early sunlight.

Above: The citrus swallowtail or Christmas butterfly.

Below: The Addo elephants tend to have small tusks; many of the females have none at all.

fenced against the larger mammals) within the Addo. The walk takes from two to fours hours, passes through unspoilt countryside and offers fine vistas and excellent game-viewing (and bird-spotting) opportunities. Day visitors have a wide choice of accommodation in the surrounding countryside and, of course, in Port Elizabeth. The Addo itself offers six-bed cottages, four-bed chalets, two-bed huts and caravan and camping sites. No accommodation is available in the Zuurberg section, though there's a hotel quite near the gate.

MOUNTAIN ZEBRA NATIONAL PARK

A Victory for Conservation

The park lies in the Eastern Cape's rugged hinterland, its landscape high-lying Great Karoo – a region where hills, lightly clothed in grasses, bush and succulents rise to become shadowy blue mountains. Highest point is the peak of Spitskop, 1,957 metres (6,419 feet) above sea level and part of the grand Bankberg range. The air is bracing, especially in winter, when the heights are capped with snow and the searing heat of summer is a distant memory.

It was on these uplands that one of the rarest of the world's large mammals, the Cape mountain zebra (*Equus zebra zebra*), was saved from extinction. In 1937, when the park was established in a great amphitheatre of the Bankberg not far from the town of Cradock, it was reckoned that there were no more than a dozen or so of these zebra still living on scattered farms, jealously guarded by concerned landowners. Today about 200 of the stocky, attractive animals graze within the protected area (which is about the optimum number it can sustain), and many others have been translocated to reserves elsewhere: a signal victory for conservation.

Smaller and lighter in weight than the plains or Burchell's zebra (*E. burchelli*), the Cape mountain zebra lacks the pale 'shadow' stripes of its more common cousin, and its legs are closely banded right down to the hooves. No two zebras, of any species, have exactly the same pattern of stripes; each coat is as individually marked as a human fingerprint.

Secure from hunters and predators, the zebra are often to be seen in the open, especially early on chilly mornings, when they make their way to east-facing slopes to stand in the sun and warm themselves. The average breeding herd – dominant male with mares and young – comprises five or six animals. A single foal is born in midsummer. Among the park's other game animals are eland, largest of southern Africa's antelope; kudu, red hartebeest, black wildebeest and blesbok. In all, 58 mammal species have been recorded within its borders. The caracal, a handsome cat, is the largest of the carnivores; birds number more than 200 species.

Getting Around

There's good game-viewing, and scenic grandeur, along the park's 40-kilometre (25-mile) road. A more adventurous option perhaps is to set out on horseback; on offer are one-hour rides. Several short hiking trails also take about an hour each to complete, while the three-day, 26-kilometre (16-mile) Mountain Zebra Trail leads you through splendid landscapes..

Staying There

The park offers four-bed self-catering cottages, a six-bed cottage and caravan and camping sites. There are two overnight huts on the Mountain Zebra Trail. Cradock has hotel and private accommodation.

Opposite, top and top right: The Cape mountain zebra, among the rarest of the world's large mammals.

Opposite, bottom left: *Aloe broomii*, one of southern Africa's 130 aloe species, is fairly common in the park.

Opposite, bottom centre: The handsome red hartebeest.

Opposite, bottom right: A watchful steppe buzzard.

Location: Eastern Cape Province, 25 km (15½ miles) west of Cradock.

Climate: Summers are scorchingly hot; winters are freezing, with snowfalls on the higher ground.

When to go: Any time of the year; the autumn and, especially, the spring months are the best.

Getting there: Cradock is situated on the N10 national highway between Port Elizabeth and Middelburg. To reach the Mountain Zebra park from Cradock, drive north from town on the N10 and, on the outskirts, turn left along the R61 for the Karoo town of Graaff-Reinet. After a further 6 km (4 miles), turn left onto the 12-km (7-mile) gravel road that leads to the park entrance. From the east, Cradock may be reached via Queenstown and Tarkastad (R61) and, from the west, via Graaff-Reinet (N9 and R61).

Facilities: Accommodation, including camping and caravan sites; restaurant; shop; conference facilities; picnic sites; swimming pool; three-day trail and short walks; horses and tack are available for hire.

Activities: The absence of the big cats and other large predators enables the park to offer horseback rides, an unusual and exciting way of seeing the wildlife. There are also hiking trails, varying from one-hour to full-day excursions, and some 37 km (23 miles) of game-viewing roads.

Wildlife: Viewing is excellent, especially on the Rooiplaat Plateau. Apart from Cape mountain zebra there are several species of large and small antelope, but no large predators or animals ordinarily regarded as dangerous to humans.

Permits and reservations: Day visitors obtain permits at the gate, but accommodation, horses and tack must be booked well in advance.

TSITSIKAMMA NATIONAL PARK

The Place of Running Water

The mountains of the southern maritime belt come close to the sea, towering above a narrow coastal plain and tapping the rain-bearing clouds that sweep in from the Indian Ocean. One of the ranges, - perhaps the most beautiful, is called Tsitsikamma, a Khoina word that recalls the sound of a rivulet, for this, these people believed, was 'the place where waters begin'. Good rains and numerous streams feed the fertile slopes and have clothed them generously in forests and fern to the very shoreline, where cliffs drop away sheer to the sea.

The rivers of Tsitsikamma are fast-flowing, and have cut immense gorges – now spectacularly bridged in places – on their short, steep journey to the ocean. Sea, shore and forest are the key ingredients of the park, a narrow, 80-kilometre (50-mile) coastal strip that ranks among South Africa's most treasured environments.

In the past the region's natural forests suffered grievously from the woodman's axe. Today, though, they are closed to exploitation, and offer a safe haven for surprisingly varied though secretive, and rarely seen, wildlife. Altogether, more than 80 different tree species thrive in the high forest (the adjective refers to the tallness of the trees, not to altitude). Many of the smaller ones have attractive foliage and scented flowers; others

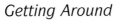

are hung with flowering creepers that grow over the young saplings and then, as these become taller, are raised with them into the sunlight. The forest floor is densely covered with fern and the low-growing shrub of the witch-hazel family called *onderbos*. Moisture, warmth and shade nurture a profusion of wild orchids, lilies and decorative fungi.

A marine reserve, runs along the park's entire length and is a paradise for snorklers and scuba-divers. The myriad rock pools of the shoreline are busy and often brilliant with marine life; giant southern right whales and schools of dolphins, often come close inshore.

Getting Around

The Otter Trail runs the full length of the park, from the headquarters at Storms River Mouth eastwards to enchanting Nature's Valley. This 48-kilometre (30-mile), five-day walk was South Africa's first organised hiking trail, and is still among the favourites. The route hugs the shore, sometimes climbing to the coastal plateau. Hikers make their way through thick forest and cross several rivers and streams, all in the most tranquil and beautiful of surroundings. There are also several short walks. The marine reserve offers an Underwater Trail.

Staying There

Cottages are set just above the rock-framed beaches near Storms River Mouth, where there are also camping and caravan sites. The park's De Vasselot section, at the western end, has two-bed 'forest huts' and camping and caravan sites. The wider area offers a variety of hotel and other comfortable accommodation.

Opposite, top: Nature's Valley, a lovely village and reserve hugged by the Tsitsikamma moutains.

Opposite, bottom left: A stream frog in contemplative mood.

Opposite, bottom right: The sun-dappled reaches of a small river that runs through the eastern end of the park.

Top right: A Cape clawless otter on the move.

Location: The park lies on the southern seaboard, about halfway between Knysna and Humansdorp.

Climate: Summer days are warm to hot; winter days often surprisingly mild, winter nights cold.

When to go: At any time. The gates are open from 5.30 am to 9.30 pm.

Getting there: From the N2 national road, turn south at the sign 9 km (5¹/₂ miles) west of the Paul Sauer Bridge that spans the Storms River.

Facilities: Near Storms River Mouth there is accommodation, a shop, restaurant and swimming pool. Several short walks and hikes start and finish at the camp.

Activities: Bird-watching; exploring the floral and intertidal marine life; angling is permitted from a section of the beach. The 48-km (30-mile) Otter Trail is a firm favourite among hikers; the Underwater Trail is a must. for snorkellers.

Wildlife: Animals are varied but not numerous; they include bushpig, baboon, vervet monkey, a few species of small antelope, caracal, leopard, Cape clawless otter. Whales and dolphins are often seen in offshore waters. Bird life includes Knysna lourie and Narina trogon.

Landscapes: Splendid sea and gorge views from the low-level suspension bridge at the Storms River estuary. The trails also offer wide vistas (except in the densely forested sections).

Permits and reservations: Day visitors obtain permits at the gate. Book accommodation well in advance through the South African National Parks (see page 174).

Precautions: If you're intent on embarking on the Otter Trail, you need to be fit, able to swim and have a good head for heights.

WILDERNESS AND KNYSNA

A Land of Lakes and Lagoons

'The most beautiful country in the universe', a pioneer naturalist called it in 1782 – and it is a description that, more than two centuries later, strikes a chord with many visitors who see this chain of tranquil, sun-dappled lakes for the first time.

The setting enchants the eye and seduces the mind. The sea is separated from the lakes by long, white beaches and a few ridges of high, bush-covered dunes; beyond, to the north, are forested slopes rising to the grand peaks of the backing Outeniqua mountains. Rivers drop swiftly down through wooded hillsides, some of them, like the Goukamma and the Kaaimans, cutting their way directly to the sea, others first flowing into limpid lagoons.

Wilderness and Beyond

The lakes region embraces seven large bodies of water and begins (if you're approaching from the west) at Wilderness, where the Touw River forms a long lagoon linked – by a winding channel called the Serpentine – to Island Lake. Then come Upper Langvlei and Rondevlei and the vast, wind-rippled surface of Swartvlei, whose dark waters are crossed by a causeway that carries a puffing, toy-like steam locomotive. Beyond the Swartvlei

Opposite, top: Canoeists paddle their way across the glassy waters of the Touw River and its lagoon.

Opposite, bottom; The entrance to Knysna Lagoon, guarded by two high sandstone cliffs known as The Heads.

Top right: Among the most colourful residents of the area's dense evergreen forests is the Knysna lourie.

estuary and the attractive little resort centre of Sedgefield is Groenvlei, sometimes called Lake Pleasant, where the deep-green water – unlike that of the other stretches – is not salty but fresh. Farther east, the Goukamma River winds through lines of scrub-covered dunes to the warm waters of the Indian Ocean. A short distance beyond is the narrow but spectacular break in the rock-bound coast where the waters of the Knysna lagoon flow, between massive sandstone cliffs known as The Heads, into the sea.

All this, contained within an area that is just 48 kilometres (30 miles) long, makes up South Africa's 'lakes district' – arguably the most attractive component of the famed Garden Route.

Three Protected Areas

The lakes, magnets for the quieter kind of holidaymaker (the area has excellent tourist facilities), are at the heart of a conservation project that embraces the Wilderness Lakes National Park, Goukamma Nature and Marine Reserve and the Knysna National Lake Area. Its nucleus is a delicate web of wetlands – lake, river and marsh – within an area of flourishing heath-type coastal fynbos that gradually merges into stretches of semi-aquatic and aquatic grasses, reeds, flowering plants and sedges. Dense patches of natural forest – ironwoods, blackwoods, and the renowned yellowwoods and stinkwoods – grace the ravines that carry the rivers down; the handsome white milkwood, a protected species, is found on the dunes and even on some of the beaches.

Above: Knysna lagoon, some 17 kilometres (10¹/₂ miles) in length, is a popular venue among yachtsmen, water-skiers and anglers.

Right: Tree ferns flourish beneath the high canopy of the Knysna forests.

The Wilderness wetlands are internationally renowned, and scientifically valued, for their bird populations: the broad stretches of water and the multitude of organisms they nurture, the dense reedbeds and a rich plant life all combine to create the ideal environment for some 200 species (of which 80 are aquatic). Notable among them are five of southern Africa's ten types of kingfisher, and the scarlet wing-flash of the brilliantly coloured Knysna lourie can (if one is lucky) be seen in the dim depths of the forest. Bird hides have been established at Upper Langvlei and Rondevlei.

Goukamma Nature and Marine Reserve includes both the estuary of the Goukamma River and fresh-water Groenvlei, tinted by the green of algae and home to a large, introduced population of black bass. Pockets of mixed milkwood, yellowwood and cherry-wood, also known as *kershout,* grow on the dunes and provide additional cover for a wealth of bird species. Giant and once endangered southern right whales make their way into the bays to mate and to calve between July and November, and can often be viewed at leisure from the shore.

The exquisite Knysna lagoon, 17 kilometres (11 miles) long and girded around by mountains and forest, is widely known and used for recreation (leisure boats ply the waters in their scores); the attractive town of Knysna hugs its shores, and the coast and surrounding countryside are fairly heavily developed. Thus the area hardly falls into the 'wild' category, but it has been carefully zoned to preserve its floral and wildlife assets. The lagoon itself is one of nature's treasure houses, noted for its birds, fish, crabs, prawns, oysters (these find their way onto the most discerning of tables), its 'pansy shells', and for the rare Knysna seahorse (*Hippocampus capensis*), which spends much of its life attached by its prehensile tail to tidal vegetation but which, despite its appearance, is a true fish.

Left: The yellowbilled duck, prominent among the birds of the wetlands.

Below: Island Lake, one of several large and limpid stretches of water that grace the Wilderness area.

Getting Around

All sections of the area are well signposted from the N2 national road, which itself has a number of lay-bys at especially scenic spots. The Passes Road was once the main route between George and Knysna; running just inland of the lakes, it bridges several rivers as it makes its way through veld and forest, offering fine views of the lovely countryside across to the lakes. Three trails have been charted; named after kingfishers and based on the Touw River area of the Wilderness park, they vary in length from three kilometres (nearly two miles) to 12 kilometres (7½ miles). A fourth, the Brown-hooded Kingfisher Trail, follows the Duiwe River from the Lakes Road. A fifth route, the Cape Dune Molerat Trail (6 km; 3½ miles) starts from the office in the bird sanctuary section of Rondevlei.

Staying There

Wilderness village, George, Sedgefield, Knysna and other centres are well endowed with hotels, guesthouses and other types of formal accommodation. Wilderness Lakes National Park maintains two rest camps on the Touw River, each offering family cottages, bungalows, huts, camping and caravan sites.

DE HOOP NATURE RESERVE

A Richly Endowed Corner of the Floral Kingdom

The dune country of this botanically important, 33,000-hectare (130 square mile) reserve, located on the southern Cape seaboard, slopes gently to the Indian Ocean, and is covered by a wealth of coastal fynbos (or, more technically, macchia), the heath-like, evergreen and flowering plant life that forms so significant a part of the famed Cape Floral Kingdom.

Altogether, the area is home to some 1,500 different floral species, of which 70 are classed as endangered and 50 grow nowhere else. The majority carry their lovely blooms in spring but De Hoop wears an attractive face all through the year. Most of the fynbos plants – the group includes the proteas and ericas – are hardy, drought-resistant perennials with woody stems and, many of them, underground storage organs (bulbs or corms).

About three kilometres (two miles) from the sea the Salt River, which runs through the reserve, has been blocked by a belt of shifting dunes to create a shallow, bird-haunted lake known as De Hoop Vlei. And the sea itself – or rather, a strip of it extending a few kilometres from the shore – has been declared a marine reserve. The vlei covers about 800 hectares (three square miles), and its fairly salty waters and reed-lined shores attract a marvellous array of waterbirds – flamingos, three species of cormorant, grebes and herons, four different kinds of duck and a host of waders and darters. Potberg, in the north, is home to Africa's southernmost breeding colony of the endangered Cape vulture.

The only indigenous fish that can tolerate the vlei's high salinity is the Cape kurper, which is remarkable for the supplementary respiratory organs that allow it to breathe out of water.

Among the reserve's 71 mammals are the bontebok and the Cape mountain zebra, both bred back from the very edge of extinction. Here you'll also find eland, largest of Africa's antelope, together with a number of smaller buck and the Cape clawless otter. Windhoek Cave houses a huge colony of bats. Another creature of the damp, dark places is the lowly and rather curious peripatus, an immensely ancient creature, resembling a velvety caterpillar, whose anatomy places it somewhere between the worms and the insects.

Whale watching from the broad white beaches or from the vantage point of a high rock brings its rewards between June and December, when the great southern right whales move close inshore, often just beyond the lines of breakers, to mate and calve. These massive marine mammals were hunted almost to extinction, but international conservation measures halted the slaughter and their numbers are now increasing by the year. In fact the offshore section is haven, from time to time, to more than a dozen different kinds of marine mammal, and its many rock pools are illuminated by a wondrous variety of marine organisms.

Opposite: The proteas, ericas and bulbous plants of the evergreen fynbos, the major vegetation of one of the world's richest, and certainly smallest, floral kingdoms, flourish on the white sands of De Hoop.

Top right: The handsome bontebok has been rescued from the very edge of extinction.

Location: On the southern coast of the Western Cape, some 60 km (35 miles) east of Bredasdorp and 193 km (120 miles) from Cape Town.

Climate: De Hoop lies in the temperate winter-rainfall region.

When to go: De Hoop is open daily from 7 am to 6 pm throughout the year. The wild flowers are brilliant in the springtime.

Getting there: From Cape Town: turn from the main N2 highway at Caledon, onto the R316 for Napier and Bredasdorp.

Facilities: Accommodation, trails, scenic drives, picnic sites with barbecue facilities.

Activities: Mountain biking; walking and hiking; bird-spotting. Whale- and dolphin-watching are an increasingly popular pastime, at its most rewarding between June and November.

Wildlife: De Hoop boasts a wide diversity of life forms, that in the marine section ranging from shellfish and tiny sandhoppers to massive southern right whales. It is also home to at least 250 species of fish. The terrestrial wildlife complement encompasses close to 60 mammals, including one of Africa's largest concentrations of the once-endangered bontebok. The bird list numbers 260 species, among them many waterbirds.

Landscapes: The wide diversity of environments and habitats includes coastal veld, beaches and a large, shallow lake.

Permits and reservations: Day visitors obtain permits at the gate, but one must book in advance for accommodation and also for the mountain bike trail. Write to The Officer-in-Charge, Private Bag X16, Bredasdorp 7280.

Above: De Hoop Vlei, the blocked lower reaches of the Sout River, attracts a wealth of waterbirds.

Below: The tail flukes of a southern right whale, seen in the marine reserve.

Right: The eland, largest of African antelope, held a special place in the lore of early Bushman hunters, who painted its image in many a rock shelter.

Getting Around

De Hoop embraces about 20 kilometres (12 miles) of scenic roads, and there are walks and hiking trails beside the shores of the lake, through the fynbos countryside and along the coast. Hikes range in length from five to ten kilometres (three to six miles). Mountain bikers can embark on routes of up to 30 kilometres (19 miles).

Staying There

In situ accommodation comprises a converted holiday home (supremely comfortable; sleeps ten; stunning seascape views), several fully furnished and equipped cottages (sleeping up to five people), camping sites and provision for educational groups. Three of the cottages are fully equipped, the others are fairly basic (take your own bedding, food and cooking utensils). The wider region, and notably Bredasdorp to the west and Swellendam to the north, offers hotels and guesthouses.

CAPE PENINSULA NATIONAL PARK

The Fairest of Lands

This, the youngest of South Africa's national parks, embraces the higher and wilder parts of the peninsula, an otherwise fairly heavily urbanized, slender finger of land that probes into the often stormy waters of the southern seas and which takes in much of Cape Town's metropolitan area.

The Cape Peninsula stretches from Table Bay southwards for nearly 60 kilometres (37 miles) to end in the rocky dagger of Cape Point. Its western seaboard confronts the great, empty spaces of the Atlantic Ocean (the nearest landfall is South America); the east coast forms part of the broad sweep of False Bay. Between False Bay and Table Bay are the low-lying Cape Flats, a sandy plain that, not too long ago on the geophysical calendar, lay beneath the sea but is now all but covered with highways, houses, shops, factories and Cape Town's big and busy international airport.

Rising sedate and supreme above all this is the peninsula's crowning glory: its cloud-wreathed mountains.

Top right: The Cape of Good Hope reserve is home to several troops of chacma baboons.

The heights extend, from the amphitheatre formed by Table Mountain and its flanking sentinels (Lion's Head and Devil's Peak), south to form the region's rugged spine. More than three centuries of expanding human presence on and around the lower slopes has left them relatively though not entirely unscathed: patches of timber forest have disappeared; alien vegetation has encroached, and much of the wildlife has become locally extinct. Nevertheless the mountains remain grand beyond measure. In some places they drop almost sheer to the sea, in others they slope away more gently to accommodate a suburb, or an expanse of parkland, or a beautifully wooded valley. Towards the southern tip the land is cut through by a wide, plateau-like plain that funnels the full blast of the ocean's winds. In summer, a gale-force southeaster often mantles the crest of Table Mountain in a 'tablecloth' of fleecy, tumbling cloud.

Mountain Fastness

The flat-topped massif of Table Mountain, one of the world's most recognisable natural landmarks, towers above Table Bay and the city of Cape Town. At its highest point – Maclear's Beacon – it reaches 1,113 metres (3,650 feet) above sea level; its straight-edge crest measures about

Location: The Penisula park is partially enclosed by the greater Cape Town metropolitan area.

Status: Application for declaration of the park as a World Heritage Site has been scheduled.

Climate: Winter rainfall area. The summer heat is tempered by the prevailing southeasterly winds; winters are wet, cool, sometimes cold.

When to go: The park (and its surrounds) have their charms whatever the season.

Getting there: Cape Town is a major tourist destination, accessible via its international airport, and by rail, road and sea (the harbour hosts a steady stream of cruise liners).

Facilities: Viewing points, picnic and barbecue sites; numerous walks and trails; leisure beaches, tidal pools. The full spectrum of tourist facilities is available just outside the park.

Wildlife: The park's mountains are home to a surprising variety and number of mammals (including baboon and leopard), reptiles and, of course, birds. Plant life is both unusual and fascinating. Larger game may be seen in the Cape of Good Hope Nature Reserve.

Landscapes: Table Mountain is world famous, but it occupies a relatively small part of the park. The other components are, in their own way, just as memorable.

Permits and reservations: Fees are payable on entry to the Cape of Good Hope and Silvermine reserves. An annual 'season ticket' is obtainable from South African National Parks' offices (see page 174).

Precautions: The weather can be treacherous on the higher slopes; don't climb Table Mountain on your own (guides are available) unless you have some experience of the area.

Above: The view south from Table Mountain takes in a series of high coastal buttresses known as the Twelve Apostles.

three kilometres (about two miles) from end to end, and on a clear day its distinctive outline can be discerned more than a 100 kilometres out to sea.

The mountain range has four faces. The precipitous northern cliff and its two flanking sentinels plunge down to meet the city; running along the western side is a series of dramatic buttresses and peaks known as the Twelve Apostles; the well-wooded southwestern face looms above the pretty little coastal town and harbour of Hout Bay, and the eastern heights look over Cape Town's older (and, in places, the city's most attractive) suburbs. The mountain determines the local distribution of rainfall: the peninsula's western areas average a modest 460 millimetres (18 inches) a year, the eastern ones, just a few kilometres away, a soggy 1,300 millimetres (50 inches) or so. The summit itself is a fine catchment area for the five upland dams that have been built.

There are more than 500 routes to the crest of Table Mountain, but the quickest and easiest way to get to the top is by cable car, a spacious, circular, windowed chamber that rotates, almost imperceptibly, as it makes its four-minute journey up from Tafelberg Road (which is at the 400-metre/1,300-foot contour). Other routes range from fairly easy walks to strenuous (and, some of them, hazardous) rock climbs. The views – of the gleaming city

far below and, beyond, of the harbour and Robben Island; of the peninsula itself, all the way to Cape Point and northwards as far as Saldanha Bay (some 90 kilometres/55 miles away) – are memorable. At the top there is a restaurant, refreshment kiosk and gift shop, telescopes, and, to help visitors to get their bearings, a toposcope. Mounted plaques describe the paths that can be followed from the cableway station and the hugely varied, and fascinating, plant life to be seen in the different seasons.

A Floral Paradise

The peninsula lies within what is known as the Cape Floral Kingdom, the botanically quite remarkable zone that extends over the relatively small winter-rainfall region of the country's southwestern and southern coastal areas. It covers a miniscule portion (0.04 per cent, to be precise) of the earth's land area yet enjoys equal status with the great Boreal Kingdom embracing North America and most of Europe and Asia. Of its 8,600 different species, around 2,600 (that is, more than the total for the whole of the British Isles) can be found on the peninsula itself. Almost all of those 2,600 grow on the mountain's slopes and on its heavily watered central plateau.

Collectively, Cape flora is known as 'fynbos' (fine bush) and embraces, for the most part, hardy, low-growing, small-leafed, drought-resistant, evergreen shrubs. Plant families such as protea (about 370 species), erica (600 species), brunia, penaea and rue are well represented. Especially varied are the proteas, which are named after Proteus, the Greek god who could change his shape at will. Notable are the king protea, South Africa's national flower; the sugar bush; and the lovely silver tree (*Leucadendron argenteum*), largest of the family. The tree grows ten metres (nearly 35 feet) tall, sometimes considerably more, and its bright, silver-haired leaves shimmer entrancingly in the Cape breezes. Among the orchids is the red disa (*Disa uniflora*), also known as 'pride of Table Mountain' and found growing along a few shady streams and in some of the deeper ravines. This floral wealth, and much more relating to the wider South African region, is on display at Kirstenbosch, on the eastern slopes of Table Mountain and regarded as one of the world's most important national botanical gardens.

Kirstenbosch is an attractively (and cleverly) landscaped area, popular among botanists, gardeners, lovers of beauty and those who like to commune with the quieter muses. Among its several specialized sections are the Cycad Amphitheatre, the Protea Garden and the Mathews Rock Garden with its profusion of succulents. Guided walks are laid on; the main paths are paved; among special features are wheelchair trails, a Braille Trail and a Fragrance Garden. There are always plants in bloom: most proteas and ericas flower in winter; daisies

The Peninsula is home to some 2,600 floral species, including watsonias (far left), leucospermums (centre; this particular one, seen growing in the Kirstenbosch gardens, grows naturally farther to the east), and the striking king protea, South Africa's national flower (above).

Left: Robben Island, with Table Mountain in the distance. The island, once a notorious 'political' prison, is now both a nature reserve and a monument to the liberation struggle.

north of Kirstenbosch, is Rhodes Memorial, a grand, temple-like granite structure that commemorates one of the more notable (and controversial) figures of the colonial era. Here there's also a tea room; superb views unfold to the east, and tame fallow deer graze under the shade of the surrounding oaks and pines. Nearby Newlands Forest is a popular venue for joggers, picnickers and strollers.

Southern Sanctuaries

Now encompassed within the park is the wild and windblown Cape of Good Hope Nature Reserve, established at the peninsula's southern tip some 60 years ago to protect the precious fynbos flora of the countryside around Cape Point. The latter, a massive headland that

Above: Boulders Beach, on the Peninsula's east coast, hosts a colony of friendly jackass penguins.

Below: The flower-filled grounds of Kirstenbosch, on the slopes of Table Mountain.

and other annuals are a blaze of colour in spring and early summer. Within the grounds are the famed Compton Herbarium, repository for more than 200,000 plant specimens; an information centre, a shop and a pleasantly informal restaurant-cum-tea room. Another favoured mountain destination, just a few kilometres

served for centuries as a crucial milestone on the long sea-route between Europe and the Indies, is not the most southerly extremity of Africa: that distinction belongs to Cape Agulhas, 145 kilometres (90 miles) to the east. Tradition, though, insists that Cape Point marks the division between the cold Atlantic and warm Indian

Left: Flowering shrubs bring subtle shades of colour to the uplands of the Silvermine reserve. Seen here are *Syncarpha vestita*.

oceans. And it is off Cape Point that the *Flying Dutchman*, the phantom ship of legend, sails forever and in vain against wind and tide.

The reserve is noted primarily for its plant life, which comprises about 1,200 different fynbos species (they put on a glorious show in springtime). But it also has its animals, the most prominent of which are the baboons that, fed (illegally) by generations of visitors, tend to be over-familiar and demanding. The area is also home to small herds of eland, hartebeest, bontebok and a few smaller antelope species.

Bird life, attracted by the mixed vegetation of fynbos, protea and milkwood, is impressive, with over 150 species recorded, and includes fish eagle and black-shouldered kite, while an entire section of beach is closed off to serve as a breeding ground of the endangered black African oystercatcher. An unusual sight is the stately parade of ostriches on Maclear beach. Just outside the reserve – at Boulders, near Simon's Town – a mainland-based colony of African black-footed or 'jackass' penguins happily coexists with beach-goers. About halfway along the length of the peninsula is the

Bottom left: The Cape grysbok, a charming though secretive resident of the Cape of Good Hope Nature Reserve.

Below: Cape mountain zebra, once a highly endangered species, have been successfully reintroduced into the reserve.

Above: Cape Town's central area huddles in a natural amphitheatre formed by Table Mountain and its flanking peaks.

Below: The rock dassie, or hyrax, a rodent-like little mammal specially adapted to life on the steep mountain slopes.

high plateau of Silvermine, an extensive and unspoilt wilderness area of woodland and heath that offers mountain walks, outstanding views over both the western and eastern seaboards, and an attractive array of avifauna (the sunbirds and sugarbirds are rather special).

The Peripheral Areas

The central uplands are well worth exploring for their scenic enchantment, and offer easy access. There is a network of short walks and trails leading from Constantia Nek, the point where the M63 (Rhodes Drive) comes to a T-junction, the road to the left leading down the scenic Hout Bay valley, that to the right into the woodland reaches of the even more lovely Constantia valley. The farms of the latter, some of them more than three centuries old, still produce fine wines even though the city's suburbs have all but enclosed them.

The peninsula and its hinterland support several bird sanctuaries. Well worth visiting is the World of Birds in Hout Bay, home to around 400 different indigenous and exotic species. Most of the 3,000 or so residents, many of them housed in walk-through aviaries, are accustomed to the human presence, and one can view and photograph them at leisure. Rather less domesticated are the 220 or so species, among them European migrants, recorded at the Rondevlei Bird Sanctuary, a stretch of marshland close to the False Bay shoreline. Best months to visit are those from February to May, but

any time spent in the hides, whatever the season, will prove rewarding. Other inhabitants of Rondevlei include hippo, steenbok, grysbok, porcupine and mongoose.

A must for nature enthusiasts is the Two Oceans Aquarium, a superb exposition of the region's marine life. It's located at the bustling Victoria and Alfred Waterfront just northwest of the city centre.

Getting Around

There are some lovely drives through and around the edges of the Cape Peninsula park. One especially scenic route, the M64 or Ou Kaapse Weg (Old Cape Road) leads you up the high Steenberg to bisect the Silvermine reserve. The vistas, across both the eastern coastal plain and, to the south, the Fish Hoek valley, are magnificent. Equally spectacular though in a quite different way is the long and winding route that follows the western shoreline from Sea Point, near the city, to the tiny hamlet of Scarborough, where you turn inland to reach Cape Point. The stretch known as Chapman's Peak Drive skirts cliffs that plunge almost sheer to the blue waters of the bay some 600 metres (2,000 feet) below.

Visitors intent on exploring the peninsula and its park, though, have a myriad options, including other scenic drives, walks and hikes, and guided tours by coach, cruise-boat, light aircraft and helicopter. Public transport is not geared to tourism, but buses do run from the city centre to Table Mountain's lower cable

station. If you plan on a walk (on this or any other mountain), get hold of a good guidebook, and heed the warning notices that have been erected along some of the paths. The region's tourism authority, Cape Town Tourism, maintains a well-appointed information centre on the city's Lower Adderley Street, and will provide guidance on walks, tours, transport and anything else the visitor needs to know.

Staying There

South African National Parks do not provide accommodation on the Cape Peninsula, but Cape Town is a modern city and offers the full spectrum of tourism facilities. Options range from the homely bed and breakfast establishment through guesthouses and flats to excellent hotels, many located at the Waterfront and along the western seaboard from Sea Point to Camps Bay.

Left: The shoreline stretching away from Cape Point. Secluded coves beckon the sunbather, the snorkler and scuba diver.

WEST COAST NATIONAL PARK

A Feast of Flowers

The storms that sweep the cold Atlantic scarcely ripple the placid surface of Langebaan lagoon, a shallow, 19-kilometre (12-mile) long, narrow expanse of water that serves as the centrepiece of a splendid wetland wilderness renowned for its bird life.

Langebaan is tucked away behind the high sheltering headlands that form the southern rampart of Saldanha Bay, one of Africa's great natural harbours but one which, because the area is dry and drinking water scarce, remained undeveloped until fairly recent times. Today Saldanha – the town lies at the bay's northern end – functions as the headquarters of the West Coast's fishing industry and its docks as a deep-sea terminal capable of accommodating the largest of bulk carriers. Among new industries attracted to the area is a huge steelworks complex. All this human activity, however, has and hopefully will continue to have little impact on the environmental integrity of this fascinating area.

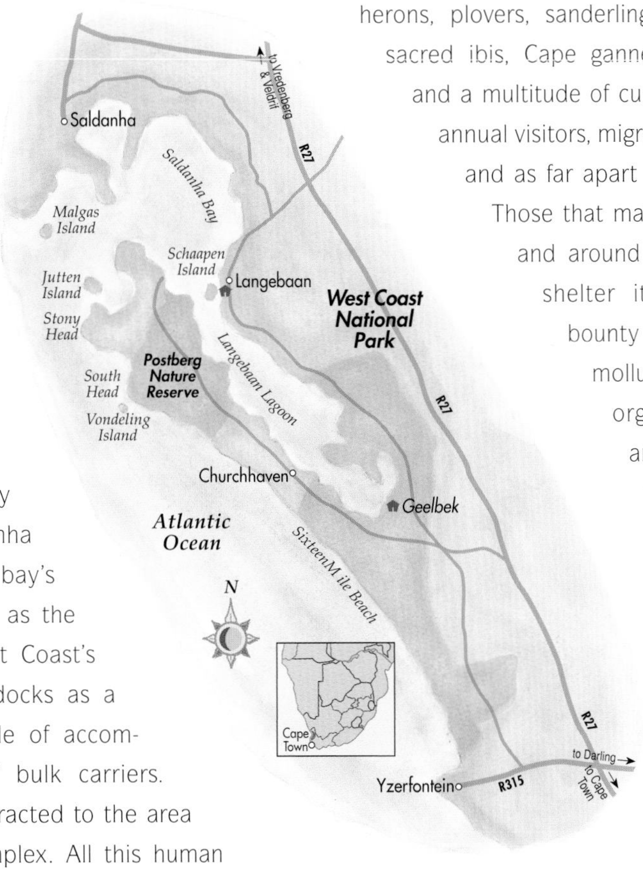

Opposite top, and top right: The glory of the West Coast. Gazanias are prominent among the flowers that mantle the park's sandy terrain for a few springtime weeks.

Opposite, bottom: Cape gannets gather in their thousands on the cliffs and offshore islands of the region.

The lagoon, the neighbouring salt marshes, mudflats and sandbanks and the rocky shores and islands of the bay combine to create one of the ornithological wonders of southern Africa. During the warm summer months a great concourse of birds gathers together – flamingos, herons, plovers, sanderlings, turnstones, knots, the sacred ibis, Cape gannets, cormorants, penguins and a multitude of curlew sandpipers. Many are annual visitors, migrants from places as remote and as far apart as Greenland and Siberia. Those that make their summer home on and around the lagoon come for the shelter it provides, and for the bounty of food – marine algae, molluscs, crustaceans and other organisms – to be found among the reedbeds and in the mud of the intertidal zone. It is estimated that Langebaan's bird population consumes more than 100 tons of these tiny creatures each year.

Land of Flowers

The West Coast National Park embraces the lagoon, the offshore islands and some 30,000 hectares (115 square miles) of the region's mostly treeless, rather bleak but, in springtime, breathtakingly beautiful maritime zone. It lies near the junction of the Sandveld and the Swartland, informal names that describe, respectively, the sandy nature of the coastal area and the dark, dense foliage that once covered the countryside inland.

Location: Saldanha Bay and Langebaan are on the Cape West Coast, 100 km (60 miles) north of Cape Town.

Climate: Temperate coastal climate, with most rain falling between May and August.

When to go: Springtime, but plan to arrive early in the morning: only limited numbers are admitted to the Postberg section at any one time.

Getting there: Follow the R27 (known as the West Coast Road) north from Cape Town for about 100 km (60 miles). The entrance to the park is west of the road.

Facilities: Walks and trails, picnic sites and amenities in Postberg, which is open only in the spring months. Tea garden and restaurant at historic Geelbek farmstead. Shops and services are available at Langebaan village and Saldanha.

Visitor activities: Watersports are a favoured pastime; bird watching; enjoying the floral wealth.

Wildlife: The lagoon is noted for its wonderful bird life, while the Postberg section (open only in spring) carries zebra, several species of antelope, and some small predators. Marine and aquatic life provide a constant source of fascination.

Landscapes: The countryside is flattish, opening up wide vistas of sea, lagoon, and the flowering veld.

Permits and reservations: A gate (to the Postberg section) is open during the spring flowering season only, when tickets are obtained on entry. One must book in advance for a place on the Sandveld Educational Trail. No crayfish (rock lobster) or abalone (perlemoen) may be caught within the park.

Precautions: Beware of strong, variable currents near Schaapen Island, where lagoon joins bay.

Map labels: to Vredenburg & Velddrif; Saldanha; Saldanha Bay; R27; Malgas Island; Schaapen Island; Jutten Island; Langebaan; Stony Head; West Coast National Park; Postberg Nature Reserve; Langebaan Lagoon; South Head; Vondeling Island; Churchhaven; R27; Atlantic Ocean; Geelbek; N; Sixteen Mile Beach; Cape Town; R27; to Darling; to Cape Town; Yzerfontein; R315

Above: The Cape cormorant, a familiar sight along the coast. Long lines of the birds in flight, or 'treks', are a common sight.

Right (centre page): Large white mussel shells litter the area's beaches.

Right: The park is bounded in the east by a rocky Atlantic shoreline.

Much of the Swartland is intensively cultivated to produce wheat, grapes and other crops, and only in patches can you see its original character. The Sandveld, however, still brings forth its own annual spring harvest of wild flowers. The flora is a mixture of the succulents common in the semiarid regions of the north, and of the blue-green Cape fynbos or macchia.

The displays are especially beautiful, and accessible, on the park's grassy Postberg peninsula, to which thousands of visitors come each year to view a kaleidoscopic tapestry of blooms with names like pigs' root, Cape dandelion, dew flower, *kalkoentjie*, sorrel and arum. In late summer, the bright red of the distinctive candelabra plant decorates the sandy flats close to the sea. When the bloom dries and falls off, the large flowerhead with its radiating spikes is tumbled about by the wind, scattering seed as it goes on its random way.

The Postberg section of the park is also stocked with large game, including zebra, eland, kudu, bontebok and several other large antelope species – an unusually and intriguing sight when viewed against their backcloth of blue sea and sandy beach.

The Distant Past

The area was once home to the very first modern humans, a fact that emerged in 1998 when archaeologists discovered sets of fossilized footprints made, in what was then wet sand, about 117,000 years ago – the earliest yet found anywhere. The theory is that the mutation which produced *Homo sapiens* occurred here, and that the new genetic form – 'Eve's' progeny – gradually spread northwards, eventually to become the world's dominant humanoid subspecies. The footprints, vulnerable to the elements and to the presence of sightseers, were lifted and flown to the South African Museum in Cape Town. At the time of writing, there were plans to create replicas of these treasures on the original site.

Other relics go back a lot further in time. Near the rail siding of Langebaan Road, 25 kilometres (15 miles) northeast of the park, quarry work has unearthed an

immense treasure-trove of fossilized life forms – marine creatures and a host of now extinct mammals – dating back about a million years. And Langebaan Lagoon itself once supported a vast oyster population, killed off at some time during the distant past by (it is thought) sudden changes in the water temperature. The lagoon's bed is overlayed by upwards of 30 million tons of their shells.

Getting Around

The park serves as both a recreational amenity and an important conservation area, and is divided into sections according to use. One zone is reserved for most water sports; another is open for most activities except power-boating and angling; a third zone is a wilderness that is closed to the public at present, and so on.

Most roads are tarred, though those in part of the Postberg section are of well-maintained gravel. The Postberg Trail (open in August and September only) runs through the game area but also offers walkers a close encounter with the quite breathtaking springtime flowers. Here, too, there is a flower trail. The two-day Sandveld Educational Trail takes in part of Sixteen-Mile Beach on the Atlantic side of the peninsula.

Visitors can embark on guided boat trips across the sheltered waters of the lagoon, or hire canoes for more leisurely do-it-yourself exploring.

Access to the off-shore islands, which are bird sanctuaries, is restricted but there are plenty of opportunities for seabird viewing from shore. Bird hides have been established near Geelbek, a gracious old (and pleasantly restored) homestead.

Staying There

Conventional (hotel and guesthouse) accommodation is available in both Langebaan and Saldanha. A six-bunk houseboat offers something different, and there are moorings for private boat-owners. Langebaan village has caravan sites and bungalows; camping is not permitted in the park itself. The Geelbek homestead provides dormitory accommodation for educational groups.

Above: The placid reaches of Langebaan Lagoon, home to a huge number and variety of waders and other waterbirds. Many are summer migrants from the Arctic wastes.

Bottom left: The handsome angulate tortoise, a species endemic to the southern tip of Africa.

Cederberg Wilderness Area

Where the Snow Protea Blooms

This extensive, scenically marvellous mountain wilderness, located about two hours' drive north of Cape Town, is famed for its strangely weathered rock formations, its cold, clear streams, its waterfalls, its ravines and peaks (Sneeuberg, its highest point, rises to 2,026 metres/6,585 feet, above sea level), its caves and overhangs and magnificent vistas. The upper slopes are home to the rare and lovely snow protea, and to the 15-metre (50-foot) tall Clanwilliam cedars themselves, while the springtime scatter of ephemeral blossoms is at its thickest and most colourful in the valleys below.

The cedars, gnarled and twisted specimens that began life a thousand years ago, are the last survivors of an almost extinct cone-bearing species, *Widdringtonia cedarbergensis*, that gave the mountains their name (the odd spelling of the area is retained from early Dutch documents). In appearance they are more like the trees of the cypress family than the classic cedars of Lebanon, which belong to the same genus as pines. Once plentiful, they have been sadly reduced over the centuries by changes in climate, by fires and by reckless over-exploitation, and today almost the only survivors are those growing high up on rocky outcrops, beyond the reach of fire.

Opposite: The 20-metre (70-foot) high Maltese Cross, one of the Cederberg's many strangely eroded rock features.

Top right: Some fine examples of ancient Bushman rock art decorate the cliff walls and caverns of the highlands.

The habitat is a harsh one – intolerably hot in summer and freezing in winter. The Cederberg, though, is rich in its own, distinctive mountain fynbos (heath-type) flora, of which the snow protea is probably the outstanding example. The underground stem of this charming little plant, protected from climatic extremes, gives the impression that leaves and flowerhead sprout directly from the soil. The species is found nowhere else in the world. More plentiful is the Cederberg or rocket protea.

A wild plant that flourishes on the Cederberg's slopes, and which is now widely cultivated for profit, is rooibos, a needle-leafed bush used to make a tannin-free and reputedly health-giving 'tea'. Another endemic species, buchu – an ingredient of many traditional medicines – produces attractive white blossoms with five wide-opening petals, and has a characteristic odour. Buchu-gatherers, some of whose families have worked the same plot or 'werf' in the mountains for generations, are still obliged to make long treks on foot to the remote and secret sites that favour their crop.

Minnows and Painted Elephants

The most often seen of the Cederberg's larger mammals is the chacma baboon, although the troops tend to keep their distance (they are not accustomed to being fed). Its arch-enemy, the leopard, also finds sanctuary in the mountains but is highly elusive, rarely revealing itself to visitors. Its presence, though, is real enough.

Numbered among the smaller mammals are caracal and wild cat, the endearing little bat-eared fox, the

Above: A carpet of bright mosses covers one of the Cederberg's upland vleis (marshy areas).

Below: A plated lizard surveys the world from its crevice home.

black-backed jackal and Cape clawless otter. Steenbok, duiker, grysbok, grey rhebok and, especially, the agile and surefooted klipspringer are at home on the rocky slopes; bird life is busy and varied, the raptor population embracing the imperious black eagle, the rock kestrel, jackal buzzard and others. The proteas of the upland slopes attract a lively array of little Cape sugarbirds and sunbirds, species with downward-curving bills designed for extracting nectar from the flowers.

The Cederberg, 71,000 hectares (275 square miles) in extent, is an important drainage area for the Olifants River, the region's major watercourse, and life in the clear, silt-free upland streams includes some rare species. Among them is the Twee Rivier redfin minnow, a pretty little fish of the *Barbus* genus with bright red markings at the base of the tail and fins. Somewhat larger is the Clanwilliam yellowfish, also restricted to the Olifants River system. The two are among eight fish species endemic to the Cederberg.

Rocks and Rock Art

Over the millennia, wind, rain and rivulet have sculpted a fantasia of strange formations from the Cederberg's sandstone, evocatively named features such the Wolfberg Arch and a deep cleft called the Wolfberg Crack; the Tafelberg and its Spout, and a 20-metre (65-foot) high pillar known as the Maltese Cross.

And then there are the caves, which have offered shelter to man and wild animal for centuries. Long-gone artists used many of them as canvasses for their remarkable paintings; fine examples of Bushman rock art are dotted throughout the Cederberg, the best known perhaps those at the Stadsaal caves. Here, elephants are depicted, with curious robed figures close by.

Elephants are now locally extinct but in fact they were common enough inhabitants of the region at one time: in the early 1700s a Dutch explorer came across a herd of at least 300 making its way along the local river, which he renamed the Olifants in their honour. The river's splendid Clanwilliam Dam serves as a prime venue for watersports and angling.

Getting Around

The Cederberg is for climbers, campers, hikers and nature lovers. Some 250 kilometres (155 miles) of well-marked footpaths criss-cross their way through the wilderness; good gravel roads lead from Clanwilliam to Stadsaal in the south, and east over the scenic Pakhuis Pass to the tiny, and supremely picturesque, village of Wuppertal. Favourite day hikes take in the most eye-catching of the rock formations; that to the Sneeuwberg peak offers attractive and in places memorable views, though the upper slopes are only for experienced climbers.

Staying There

Various grades of accommodation are available on the area's private farms; Cape Nature Conservation offers caravan and camping sites (notably around the Algeria Forest Station); there are camping sites at Kliphuis, and roofed accommodation at Waenhuis and Uitkyk. Clanwilliam and Citrusdal have hotels. Trailists overnight in basic huts.

Above: The *Disa uniflora*, also known as Pride of Table Mountain, is part of the Cederberg's lovely floral tapestry.

Bottom left: One of the area's more striking rock formations is the Wolfberg Arch.

NAMAQUALAND AND RICHTERSVELD

A Wonderland of Wild Flowers

Location: Springbok is 550 km (340 miles) north of Cape Town.

Climate: Hot and dry, although winter nights are cold. Dew is heavy near the coast; nighttime and dawn mists roll in from the sea.

When to go: The flowers are usually at their brief best in early spring (September).

Getting there: From Cape Town, drive north on the N7; from Gauteng, on the N14 via Upington and Pofadder. Most motorists get to the Richtersveld park via Steinkopf, Port Nolloth, Alexander Bay and Reuning.

Facilities: Full facilities are available in Namaqualand's main centres. The Richtersveld park offers limited accommodation (most visitors set up camp), scenic routes (for 4x4s) and, from 1 April to 30 September, guided trails of up to four days.

Landscapes: The sheer ruggedness of the region, and especially of the Richtersveld, is a major attraction, but most visitors come for the breathtaking floral cover.

Permits and reservations: These are required in the Richtersveld only, where admission and overnight permits must be obtained from the park headquarters at Reuning. Trails and cottages should be reserved well in advance through the South African National Parks (see page 174). Local permission is usually granted for the use of private roads during the flower season; general information can be obtained from the Tourist Information Office, Springbok, and from the Tourism Gateway Centre in Cape Town's lower Adderley Street. For the latest update on the best floral displays during the season, ring Flowerline on (021) 418 3705.

Precautions: Carry water, extra fuel and all other requirements when travelling in the Richtersveld.

The western coastal strip to the south of the Orange River is a harsh, heat-seared, unforgiving land where, for much of the year, almost the only green to meet the eye is the tint that hardened mineral salts create on the wrinkled surface of the hot granite. The earth is reddish and bone dry, the sun burns relentlessly from the unbroken blue of the sky, and scanty herds of livestock range far and wide in their quest for nourishment. To the casual observer it seems one of the least generous of landscapes – until spring, when it is mantled, suddenly, in a brilliant, bewildering tapestry of wild desert flowers.

This is Namaqualand, that part of the Western and Northern Cape provinces whose sandveld flanks the Atlantic Ocean and extends inland for some 50 kilometres (30 miles) to the broken country of the Hardeveld and, beyond, the semi-arid wastes of Bushmanland. The farther south one travels, the more generous the land becomes until one crosses the Olifants River to reach Clanwilliam, Citrusdal and the grand heights of the Cederberg (see page 89).

Namaqualand's principal town is Springbok, which lies on the N7 national road some 550 kilometres (340 miles) north of Cape Town and is the ideal base from which to explore the region. Nearby are the small copper-mining centres of Nababeep and Okiep.

The area drew the interest of the Dutch settlers during the latter part of the 17th century, when travellers saw that the local Nama people wore copper ornamentation, but nearly two centuries were to pass before the inaugural mine made its appearance. Much later, in the 1920s, the Sandveld to the west yielded its first diamonds, discoveries that led to the charting and exploitation of some of the world's richest alluvial fields. They are served by the coastal towns of Port Nolloth and Alexander Bay.

Surviving the Seasons

Rain is the 'shy stranger' of Namaqualand, averaging less than 250 millimetres (10 inches) a year. In many places it falls below 50 millimetres (2 inches) or less, and everywhere sinks quickly away into the parched earth. Nevertheless, despite the hostility of the land, the aridness, the intense heat and the poverty of the soils, the wider region sustains an incredible 4,000 and more different species of plant.

Like that of the Skeleton Coast far to the north (see page 117), the flora of the coastal Sandveld gets its precious moisture from the nightly mists that swirl in from the cold ocean. The actual amount of water is minimal, but Namaqualand's plants are superbly adapted to

Opposite, far left: Among Namaqualand's floral delights are Lachenalia (top) and Bulbinella or cat's tail (centre); wildlife includes the angulate tortoise (bottom).

Opposite, right: The weird 'halfmens' or 'elephant's trunk' tree, a succulent common in the Richtersveld park.

Top right: Daisies brighten the dusty earth for a few weeks.

survive droughts that sometimes last for years. Many of them, here and in the arid inland areas, are succulents of one kind or another, perennial plants that store water in their stems and leaves – and keep it from evaporating (or transpiring) in the hot sun with the help of their deep pores (or stomata), their thickened leaf-skins and coverings of wax, hairs or leaves. The surfaces of the leaves and stems may also be reduced, so that the area that is exposed to sun and wind is minimized. Geophytes – plants that form buds below the soil surface – survive the hot summers as bulbs, corms or tubers. Their two large leaves, lying flat on the ground, create their own micro-climate by lessening evaporation from the soil. Those shrubs with large, free leaves, though, shed them during summer to prevent too much water loss.

The most exquisite of Namaqualand's massed flowers are the ephemerals, annual plants stirred into sudden germination and growth by a combination of life-giving elements – gentle winter rain followed by the slow warming of the earth, the coming of the desert breezes and the arrival of the pollinators. They flaunt their glorious flowerheads – of orange, yellow or white – in a wondrous display and then, within just a few weeks, die back to disappear until the next spring.

The Land in Flower

Perennials are among the first prominent flower groups to catch the eye on your springtime drive north from Cape Town, both along the main N7 highway (inland) and the R27 (coastal) route. These are the *vygies* or sour figs, members of the huge and enormously varied mesembryanthemum group of plants. Some of the many and various species you'll see are bushy, others sprawl haphazardly across sand dunes. Their blaze of glittering colours is a foretaste of Namaqualand in bloom, although the spectacle varies in its nature and extent from year to year depending on how generous the winter rains have been, and on whether or not the flowers have been subjected to the hot winds.

Namaqualand proper starts beyond Klawer and Vredendal on the Olifants River, though these two towns can be included in a circular drive that also takes in Clanwilliam, Lutzville and the attractive little coastal centre and fishing harbour of Lambert's Bay. The route covers a rewarding part of the sandveld, an area where plants such as pale yellow grielum, and wild flax drink from the mist. Clanwilliam, moreover, is an excellent base from which to explore the floral wonders of the high Cederberg and the lovely Biedouw Valley, while the

Below: The dassie rat is one of the species of rock mice (*Petromyscus*) that live in crevices in southern Africa's more arid parts.

Above: More than 355 species of wild flower have been recorded in the Skilpad ('Tortoise') Wildflower Reserve near Kamieskroon.

Vanrhynsdorp and Calvinia areas are also noted for their fine displays, and, especially, for their many varieties of endemic lithops, or stone plant.

Further north you'll see some larger, curious-looking species – the sentinel-like, vaguely humanoid halfmens tree (*Pachypodium namaquanum*) for example, and aloes that include the kokerboom or quiver tree. The latter is so named because the Bushmen (or San) used to fashion receptacles for their arrows from its bark.

Northwards again and inland is the hilly plain known as the Knersvlakte, part of the Hardeveld, whose red sands are covered with small, white quartz pebbles and dominant growths of *vygie*s. Also embraced by the Hardeveld is the Klipkoppe, an area of rocky hills whose higher parts, blessed with as much as 400 millimetres (16 inches) of rain a year, are – some of them – clothed in evergreen heath-type flora known as fynbos. A prominent species here is the white-flowered shrub called *kapokbos*, which belongs to the family Asteaceae, a very large floral group that includes the famous

Namaqualand 'daisies' among its members. These are low-growing shrubs whose flowers have a flattish, circular centre and radiating yellow, white or orange petals.

It is the immense quantity of flowers and sheer variety of species that amaze the visitor to Namaqualand, but the great tapestries that mantle plain and hill to the far horizons are, for the most part, woven from just a few types: yellow *Dorotheanthus oculatus*, purple *Drosanthemum hispidum* and yellow *Grielum* species, though sometimes the bright orange of the double Namaqualand daisy, *Arctotis fastuosa*, may be the dominant colour; elsewhere there are flower-lakes of blues and whites and other colours in an endless variety of shades. Even the unpromising rocks are garlanded with floral chains that have, somehow, found an unlikely root-hold. Some of the best displays can be seen on farmland.

Viewing the flowers is not as simple and straightforward a pleasure as it might seem. The blooms are opened by warmth and light, so most species don't show their faces until mid-morning and will probably close well before sunset. And, when open, they face the strongest light, so if you are driving toward the sun you will not see them at their best. It is recommended that you stop frequently to look around and behind you.

Richtersveld National Park

This vast wilderness, bounded on three sides by a great loop of the Orange River, occupies the far north and is the harshest part of Namaqualand. Its own northern section is hilly, desolate, distinguished by strangely sculpted rock formations and bare, bone-dry plains; its southern is covered in scrub and sparse grassland. The area receives almost no rain, and summer temperatures sometimes climb to more than 50° centigrade (120° fahrenheit). Winter nights, though, can be bitter. Plants, mammals, insects, birds and reptiles rely for life-sustaining moisture on fogs that creep in from the Atlantic Ocean on most nights.

The Richtersveld is what is known as a 'contractual park', an arrangement in terms of which the local Nama inhabitants, stock herders for the most part, retain their residential, grazing and other rights and are involved in the management of the area.

Despite unpromising conditions, the park boasts a remarkable range of wildlife and floral (especially succulent) species – indeed, it is home to fully one third of all the world's known kinds of mesembryanthemum Quiver trees and the bizarre halfmens are common sights. Notable, too, is the bird life, which is prolific: more than 180 species have been recorded. Game includes the rarely seen Hartmann's mountain zebra, several kinds of antelope, baboon, vervet monkey, leopard and caracal. Reptiles are also present in moderate numbers.

This challenging mountain desert is not really for the casual visitor. Roads are tracks and, although ordinary vehicles with high ground clearance (such as combis and LDVs) may manage some of them, sedan cars are not allowed entry. Four-wheel drives, and driving in convoy, are more or less obligatory.

Getting Around

Almost all the flower-route roads – including the private ones – are suitable for the ordinary sedan car. Especially rewarding are those to and through Leliefontein in the mountains above Garies; Spektakel Pass; Komaggas; the area west of Kamieskroon, and Kamiesberg Pass. The Hester Malan Wildflower Garden, in the Goegap Nature Reserve just outside Springbok, is an excellent reference area. As mentioned, you'll need a 4x4 to explore the harsh spaces of the Richtersveld.

The flowers are usually at their best in August and September. Before setting out on an exploratory foray, contact Flowerline on toll-free 0800 00 1704 or Cape Town (021) 418 3705 during the season, or call in at Cape Town's tourist information centre in Lower Adderley Street (near the railway station), for pointers to the most rewarding viewing areas.

Staying There

Springbok and other towns offer hotel or guesthouse accommodation. Many of the local farmers provide pleasant room and board, and, as important, advice on where and when to see the best displays. Richtersveld National Park has ten-, eight- and four-bed cottages (bedding and towels supplied) with fully equipped kitchens, and several small camping sites.

Above: A malachite sunbird rests on *Leucospermum reflexum*, one of Namaqualand's myriad species of wildflower. The bird is widely distributed in southern Africa.

Below, left: Many plants of the pedaliaceae, or sesame, family have tubers valued for their medicinal properties, but carry spiny fruits that pose a danger to grazing animals.

Below: Cape francolin, also called Cape pheasant, nest on the ground, producing large clutches of up to ten eggs.

KALAHARI GEMSBOK NATIONAL PARK

Life in the Great Thirstlands

The Nossob River and its tributary, the Auob, run southwards, cutting wide valleys through the high dunes of red Kalahari sand. Only rarely, though, does water flow in their beds, which are graced for long stretches by the green of grass, shrubs and stately camelthorn trees, all drawing moisture from far below the surface. These riverbeds are so reliably dry – the Auob runs about once in each decade, the Nossob once a century – that they serve as excellent routes into and across this huge, arid, mostly desolate, sometimes surprisingly beautiful land.

The region is termed a desert because of its sandy, porous soils, low rainfall and lack of surface water, but in reality it is a wilderness, an immense, usually bone-dry country of regimented dunes and, towards the north, great plains covered in scanty but sweet grasses that sustain a wealth of game animals and their predators. When the rare rains come (at any time between December and April) the harsh landscape takes on a mantle of greenery almost overnight, and for a brief week or so resembles nothing so much as lush parkland.

Opposite, top: A skeletal camelthorn tree bows down beneath the lowering Kalahari sky.

Opposite, bottom left: A Cape fox pup emerges, bright-eyed from the burrow in which it rests for most of the day.

Opposite, bottom right: A pair of yellow mongooses forage for the insects that form the major part of their diet.

Top right: Suricates, locally known as meerkats, warm themselves in the sun while staying alert for enemies.

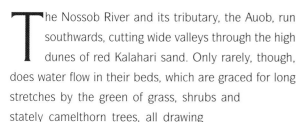

On the map, the park forms a wedge pointing southeast from the Namibian frontier and contained between the two rivers. Across the Nossob is Botswana, with its own Gemsbok National Park (*see* page 151), the combined conservation area extending across more than 3,6 million hectares (14,000 square miles). There are no fences between the two, and the game is free to trek – which it sometimes does en masse and in spectacular fashion. The two areas are being brought under unified control to form southern Africa's first transnational or 'Peace Park'. During the long droughts the animals and birds get their water from boreholes, the first of which were sunk in the riverbeds in 1914, when the South African forces thought of invading the then German colony of South West Africa from this region. It was this, rather than roads, that opened the area to travellers and, eventually, to the hunters who took so heavy a toll of the game – until 1931, when the park was proclaimed a sanctuary.

The Game Herds

The Kalahari is home to the gemsbok, sturdy relative of the Arabian oryx and seen in herds of a dozen or more when grazing is good but in smaller groups when food is scarce. This handsome and powerful antelope is most easily recognised by the V-shaped arrangement of its straight, tapering horns. The animal is supremely well adapted to desert conditions: it scarcely ever drinks, obtaining its moisture from the wild melons that grow in the wilderness, and from succulent roots and bulbs. Moreover, its physiology is so designed that it has no

Location: The park occupies the northwest corner of the Northern Cape Province (it is wedged between the Namibia and Botswana borders) 260 km (160 miles) from the town of Upington and 900 km (560 miles) from Johannesburg.

Climate: Hot (over 40° Centigrade (104° Fahrenheit) in summer) and dry. Winter nights can be freezing.

When to go: April to May, when daytime temperatures are beginning to moderate, are best for general game-viewing. Gates are open from sunrise to sunset. Busiest periods are the school holidays.

Getting there: Most people arrive by road via the R360, which turns off the N10 between Upington and Namibia. Twee Rivieren's airstrip is used by fly-in visitors.

Facilities: An information centre, restaurant, pool at Twee Rivieren. Shops at all three camps sell fuel, firewood and groceries (fresh food only at Twee Rivieren).

Wildlife: Among the antelope species are gemsbok, eland, springbok, red hartebeest and eland; blue wildebeest are fairly prominent; carnivores include black-maned lion, leopard, cheetah, caracal, spotted and brown hyaena, black-backed jackal and honey badger (ratel). Bird life is surprisingly varied; the raptors are especially impressive.

Permits and reservations: Book well in advance of your visit, through the South African National Parks (see page 174).

Precautions: The Kalahari Gemsbok National Park is a low-risk malaria area. Keep your shoes on at night in summer, and especially during hot, windy periods (a precaution against scorpion stings).

Above: The leopard is a powerful hunter and a versatile one, able to seize an antelope more than twice its size and weight but happy to take mice when nothing else is available.

Below: The scaly, ant-eating pangolin, here seen scurrying for safety across the red sand of the Kalahari, is rarely observed by day.

Bottom right: Although deadly, the Cape cobra is a shy creature, preferring to avoid confrontation.

need to perspire. It has a built-in mechanism (an unusual though not unique one) that controls the temperature of the blood flowing to its brain – a vital aid to survival in this harsh, searingly hot land.

The southern Kalahari's other antelope, which are also adapted to withstand the long droughts, include the red hartebeest, the blue wildebeest, the eland and the versatile springbok, South Africa's national animal.

These last are both browsers and grazers (they will even dig up bulbs and roots) and rank among the fastest and most agile of all Africa's mammals: they are able, when hard pressed, to gallop along at a breathtaking 90 kilometres (55 miles) an hour, covering the ground in huge, 15-metre (33-foot) bounds. They also go through a sequence known as 'stotting', a series of high, stiff-legged leaps with arched back – a strange behavioural display which remains improperly understood. Early travellers recorded periodic migrations in such numbers that a column of packed springbok, estimated to be about a kilometre wide, took more than two hours to pass by. The conversion of the countryside to commercial farming, and the erection of fences in the surrounding ranchlands, make it unlikely that a springbok 'trek' will ever be seen anywhere but in the Kalahari, and even there the mass movements are rare and comparatively modest in terms of numbers.

The Carnivores

Among the park's large predators is the lion, here distinguished by the black manes of the adult males – a distinctive local variation (though the animals are otherwise no different from lions elsewhere in southern Africa).

Like the Kalahari's other creatures, however, the mighty lion has had to adjust its life style to the harsh realities of terrain, climate and limited food resources. Large prey animals are relatively scarce, and the lightly covered countryside favours the hunted rather than the hunter. In order to stay alive, therefore, the big cat must range widely and settle for more modest prey than is usual in most other big-game sanctuaries. A Kalahari lion has to make around 50 kills a year to remain in reasonable shape – more than three times as many as its cousins in the Kruger National Park. And at least half its kills are small mammals, which make up just one per cent or so of a Kruger lion's diet.

More successful, perhaps, are the park's spotted hyaenas, a species much maligned in legend and myth, popularly perceived as a lowly scavenger that feeds on the left-overs of nobler animals. In reality the hyaena is a remarkable species, tough, self-sufficient, supremely opportunistic. It does scavenge, of course, but it is also a resourceful hunter, living and operating in a loose-knit clan led by a matriarch. Other Kalahari carnivores include leopard, caracal, brown hyaena, black-backed jackal, bat-eared fox (which eats insects) – and, most notably, the graceful and streamlined cheetah, swiftest of all land mammals. The Nossob and Auob river beds, which sustain relatively large numbers of springbok, provide a far better home for cheetah than most other African habitats – and, because the vegetation is so sparse, they offer the visitor superb viewing

Above centre: A natural white 'eye-liner', visible below this lioness's eye, reflects and intensifies available light at night, making the African lion one of the most formidable of nocturnal hunters.

Above right: Unlike the lion, the swift and graceful cheetah is essentially a daytime hunter. The dark 'teardrop' marks on the animal's face absorb the harsh daylight and help to reduce glare.

Left: Gemsbok bulls fence tentatively with their lance-like horns, preparing for the day when they will challenge for leadership.

Above: A springbok leaps into the air in one of the high, stiff-legged actions known as 'stotting' or 'pronking'. The reason for this behaviour is not known, but may be prompted by sheer *joie de vivre*.

Right: Barking geckos carry their bodies clear of the burning Kalahari sand. These are the only lizards that can produce a sound other than a simple hiss.

Below: The stately bateleur, which has a distinctively short tail beyond which its feet protrude in flight. The bird is one of nature's most spectacular acrobats.

opportunities, perhaps the best in the world. Moreover, these particular animals, shy elsewhere, co-operate in the viewing process, habitually ignoring the presence of humans and their vehicles.

Smaller but just as fascinating in their routines are the honey badger (also known as the ratel), the rarely seen antbear (more commonly known in South Africa as the aardvark) and aardwolf, and those endearing sun-loving burrowers, the ground squirrel and the suricate.

Bird Life

Altogether, around 200 bird species have been recorded within the park. In volume terms it is reckoned that almost one fifth of the area's birds are raptors, hunting and feeding on anything from insects to small mammals. Among the most regal are the martial and tawny eagles. Notable, too, is the lappet-faced vulture which, although primarily a scavenger, will also hunt and kill small mammals and young birds. The adult boasts a wingspan of more than 2½ metres (eight feet) and will soar and glide quite magnificently on the rising air currents.

Getting Around

Two good gravel roads, negotiable in an ordinary family saloon, follow the course of the Nossob and Auob rivers, and are linked by two tracks: between the Kamkwa and Dikbaardskolk and the Auchterlonie and Kij Kij picnic spots. A private safari operator, based outside the park but contactable through the park's office, takes visitors on an exhilarating 4x4 dune trail.

Do not wander off the beaten paths: you're quite likely to get stuck in the soft sand. Some stretches can be very challenging during the rainy season. Before setting off, check with the camp authorities about the latest sightings: they are in contact with one another by radio and can provide the very latest information.

Staying There

The park's main camp and administrative headquarters are at Twee Rivieren, located on the southern boundary. There are two smaller camps: Nossob, on the Nossob River, and Mata Mata on the Auob. The three camps offer a pleasant mix of six-, four- and three-bed huts; Twee Rivieren's are airconditioned. All the camps have caravan and camping sites (without power points). Twee Rivieren also offers a restaurant and swimming pool; each camp has its own shop.

Right: Blue wildebeest travel great distances to find new grass and fresh, clean water.

AUGRABIES FALLS NATIONAL PARK

Canyon and Cascade

Augrabies is derived from the local Korana word Oukurubi, which means (roughly) 'the place of great noise' or 'the hollow place' – an apt enough name for one of the world's great waterfalls. It is here, on the southern fringes of the Kalahari, that the Orange River, on its 2,188-kilometre (1,360-mile) journey westwards from the highlands of Lesotho to the Atlantic Ocean, plunges through an immense, 18-kilometre (11-mile) long granite gorge whose sides, in some places, drop nearly 100 metres (more than 300 feet) down to the roaring waters below.

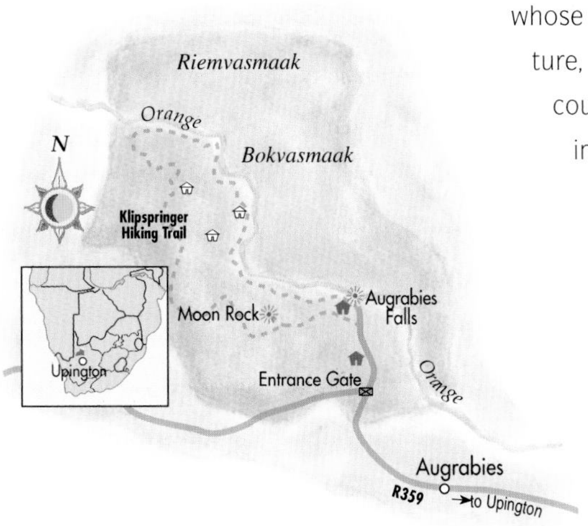

When the river is in high flood, there may be up to 19 different falls with a total volume of more than 400 million litres (90 million gallons) crashing over the rim of the main section each minute. At these times the noise is overwhelming, the air hung with fine rainbow-threaded mists. The water drops straight down for almost 90 metres (200 feet, 120 of which are freefall) into a deep, mysterious, rock-enclosed pool. At the bottom of the pool, some say, is a fortune in diamonds washed down by the river over the centuries. Rumour also has it that the fabled Kruger millions are hidden here, but the guardianship of the great river and of a vaguely described 'monster' keeps all secrets safe. The latter is

Top right: Blunt, rubbery hooves give the klipspringer the grip that makes it such an assured and graceful jumper in high, rocky places.

supposed to have devoured cattle that wandered along the riverbed during a dry spell in the 1930s, but scientists say there's probably nothing more sinister here than a giant barbel and some tall stories.

The falls are the centrepiece of an 23,000-hectare (90-square mile) park whose Moon Rock, a prominent feature, aptly describes the Augrabies countryside – or at least the first impressions it imparts. The rock is a bald granite dome which provides fine views over the rugged landscapes running away both to the north and south of the river's banks. The park's headquarters are located on Klaas Island.

Vegetation is sparse, but camelthorns and the kokerboom or quiver tree *(Aloe dichotoma)* thrive along the river, supplying what little shade there is. Most of the smaller plants are succulents, such as the aloes, which store precious water in their specially adapted leaves and stems. Wildlife includes springbok and the sure-footed klipspringer, gemsbok, giraffe, leopard, baboon, vervet monkey – and, perhaps most notably, the endangered black rhino. The park is also known for the number and variety of its reptiles.

Getting Around

Guided outings are among the highlights of a visit to Augrabies. The Black Rhino Adventure starts with a rubber-duck ride to the north bank, from where a 4x4 day-safari, with field guide and tracker, sets off in search of black rhino, the local, arid-adapted subspecies of

Location: The park lies some 110 km (70 miles) west of Upington in the semiarid Northern Cape.

Climate: Days are warm to very hot throughout the year; winter nights are very cold. Rain falls from January through to April, but, locally, rarely amounts to more than an annual 200 mm (8 inches).

When to go: March to October are the most pleasant months. The river is at its highest between October and January. Gates close at 10 pm.

Getting there: From Upington: drive west for approximately 110 km (70 miles) on the N14 and turn right 8 km (5 miles) after passing Kakamas. From Cape Town, take the N7 to Springbok and then travel northeast on the N14. Upington can be reached via the N14 from Johannesburg and Pretoria. The town is a scheduled stop for the national airline.

Facilities: Accommodation, shop, restaurant, swimming pools. Mountain bikes and canoes for hire. Game-spotting safaris. The main viewing site at the falls is enclosed by a safety fence.

Wildlife: The north bank has been restocked with black rhino, giraffe, zebra and several large antelope species, all of which are accessible via the guided rhino tours. Birds, reptiles and insects.

Landscapes: The falls themselves are the centre of attraction, but the barren-looking countryside and its wildlife merit exploration.

Permits and reservations: Accommodation and a place on the Klipspringer Hiking Trail must be booked in advance. Day visitors can obtain permits at the gate.

Precautions: Stay behind the safety fences, both at the main falls and elsewhere along the gorge.

Map labels: Riemvasmaak · Orange · N · Bokvasmaak · Klipspringer Hiking Trail · Moon Rock · Augrabies Falls · Upington · Entrance Gate · Orange · Augrabies · R359 · to Upington

Above: The Orange River, on its way through the thirstlands, tumbles over the Augrabies falls.

Above, top right: The black rhino, in contrast to its white cousin, rarely eats grass: its tapering upper lip is adapted for browsing on leaves and twigs.

Above, bottom right: The sun-loving rock dassie. This little animal's closest relative is the elephant.

which (classified as *Diceros bicornis bicornis*) copes well with the climate and bare, dry terrain. Here, too, the endangered animal is relatively safe from poachers.

More strenuous is the three-stage odyssey that involves a canoe paddle on the mighty Orange, a hike, and an 11-kilometre (seven-mile) ride by mountain bike back to base camp. This is a personal challenge rather than a game-viewing trip, but it's a great way to enjoy the park. Everything you'll need – right down to life jackets and maps – is provided. Straightforward walks and hiking trails are other options; rather special is the three-day, 26-kilometre (16-mile) Klipspringer Trail, a south-bank route that takes in Moon Rock and Ararat (from which there are magnificent gorge views). The trail is closed between October and March due to the searing heat. There are also the more conventional means of sightseeing: one can embark on self-guided drives along the well-maintained gravel roads.

Staying There
The park offers fully serviced, four-bed cottages with air conditioning, and two three-bed cottages adapted for handicapped visitors. The caravan and camping sites are equipped with power points.

Left: The waters of the Orange River in flood dwarf an adventurous visitor to the Augrabies Gorge.

Below: A dead quiver tree in the dry vastness of the Augrabies area. The species, an aloe, received its rather unusual common name from its value to early Bushman hunters, who used its bark to make quivers in which to carry their poisoned arrows.

NAMIBIA

The young Republic of Namibia, independent only since 1990, occupies some 823,000 square kilometres (320,000 square miles) of sparsely populated, sand-blown, mostly barren-looking countryside sandwiched between South Africa and Angola in the arid western quadrant of the subcontinent. It has been described as 'a land God made in anger', and indeed there is a hint of elemental fury in the reefs and racing currents of the Skeleton Coast, in the jagged harshness of the interior uplands, in the immense desolation of the Namib Desert. But there is life, even in the wildest of the wastelands, and a haunting scenic beauty which is quite unlike that of any landscapes anywhere else. The rare rains fall only in the summer months, when the temperatures in some areas (in the Orange River valley, for instance) may reach 48° Centigrade (118° Fahrenheit), although the capital, Windhoek, situated on the country's relatively high central 'spine', enjoys a pleasantly moderate climate. Even cooler are the coastal centres, whose air is chilled by an ocean current that brings water north from the polar regions. For the most part plant life, well adapted to desert conditions, comprises succulent species in a diversity of bizarre forms; in the dry coastal areas, lichens are almost the only vegetation, their habitats ranging from mist-shrouded shores and long, lonely beaches inland to sand dunes and rock-strewn plains.

The far northern part of the country enjoys more generous rains, its river system bringing precious water to the great Etosha Pan and the relatively lush game reserves of Caprivi. Wildlife is surprisingly abundant, even outside the formally protected areas, and some of it is found in unexpected places – elephants in the desert, for instance, and jackals on the beaches. Many of the smaller species, notably the reptiles and insects, have evolved in quite remarkable fashion to survive the rigours of Namibia's climate and terrain. Travel to and within Namibia is relatively free of problems. Air services (scheduled and charter) are sophisticated; a well-maintained highway runs south-north, across the central plateau, to and beyond Windhoek; and tarred roads lead to most places of interest, though you will need a 4x4 if you intend straying from the main routes.

Left: The harsh, lonely and often hauntingly beautiful landscapes of Namibia are home to a surprising variety of animal and plant life.

Above: The well-camouflaged Namaqua chameleon is among the larger members of its family.

FISH RIVER CANYON

A Moonscape of Chasms

At first glance it seems that the rocky plains of southern Namibia have baked too long in the scorching African sun, and that the very crust of the earth has cracked wide open to create a great, gaping, 160-kilometre (100-mile) gorge that ranks among the continent's most awesome natural wonders. Sheer cliffs expose strata of water-laid sediments layered all the way down to its granite floor, 550 metres (1,800 feet) below (in places) and 2,500 million years distant in time.

It was an ancient sea that created this sequence of rocks, mostly soft shales and sandstones, and it was a river – violently in flood over the millennia – that carved the canyon. Now the flow has diminished (though tumultous floodwaters still, occasionally, sweep through), and for much of the year the riverbed holds little but a scatter of glistening seasonal pools. Near the canyon's southern rim is a powerful, gushing spring of scalding hot water.

The Fish River rises near the Naukluft mountains and, in February and March, its rain-fed waters wind their way 800 kilometres (500 miles) southwards to join the Orange River, which marks the border between the republics of Namibia and South Africa. Some two thirds of the way along its course it cascades over one cliff and then another before entering its gigantic gorge.

Stand close to the precipice at the viewsite above Hell Bend and you'll see before you a scene of quite magnificent desolation: the great canyon, in parts as much as 27 kilometres (17 miles) wide, has been carved into a spectacular, maze-like moonscape of plunging chasms. Few vistas in Africa, or indeed anywhere else, can match the grandeur of this place. It is especially memorable at dawn and at sunset, when the changing light flushes the gaunt rocks and soaring cliffs with an infinite subtlety of colour.

For part of the way there are really two canyons, one within the other. The wider one is the older, cut through the softer surface sediments, but a later earth movement caused the river to flow faster, and it carved a second, deeper channel in the bed of the first, gradually, over the aeons, forming the gorge's present configuration.

The Long Trail

From your high vantage point you can sometimes observe, far below, tiny, ant-like creatures making their way slowly downstream. These are hikers, tackling one of southern Africa's most challenging trails.

Opposite: The immense and lonely spaces of the Fish River Canyon were shaped, over countless millennia, by the action of wind and water. Some of the rocks are more than two billion years old.

Top right: The quiver tree, a species of aloe, grows to about five metres (16 feet). Its scientific name, *Aloe dichotoma*, refers to the simple arrangement of its network of branches, each of which splits into two.

Location: The canyon cuts through the extreme southern part of Namibia, west of the main B1 highway. It forms part of the wider Ai-Ais Hot Springs Game Park.

Climate: Hot (often very hot) and dry, but nights may be cool, even cold, at any time of the year, but especially in the winter months.

When to go: Ai-Ais resort is closed from November to mid-March because of excessive heat and the possibility of flooding. Hiking in the canyon is permitted only from May to September.

Getting there: Some 37 km (23 miles) north of Viooolsdrif, turn west off the B1 onto the D316 for Ai-Ais Hot Springs. From the north, turn west onto the R97 (C10) 33 km (21 miles) after passing Grunau.

Facilities: Ai-Ais has shops, restaurant, bar, fuel, swimming pool, tennis court and many other facilities. There is no bank.

Equipment: Take your own crockery and cutlery if you are staying at Ai-Ais. Take all your own camping equipment, including warm clothing or bedding, light fishing gear (just for the challenge), a shade hat and barrier cream.

Wildlife: Birds are the most visible of the canyon's living forms; mammals are present but shy.

Landscapes: The scenery can be enjoyed both from the gorge's rim and its floor. The sunrise and sunset hours are magical.

Permits and reservations: Book through the Namibian Directorate of Tourism and Resorts (see page 174) for the Fish River Canyon Trail, and remember to supply a valid form of medical fitness not more than 40 days prior to the start date. An admission fee is charged at Ai-Ais.

Above: Pied kingfishers are most often seen in pairs, on a perch overlooking water. For the most part their diet consists of tiny shellfish, fish and insects.

Right: Splendid vistas unfold from the summit of the gorge.

date palms provide cool, green shade. It is said that the trees were planted by German prisoners-of-war who, in 1916, escaped and hid for months in this lonely corner of the country. Vegetation is sparse, and, apart from poolside reeds, is confined to grasses and scrubby bush, succulents and a few small trees. Bird life, though, is abundant, especially around the pools, where sociable weavers have built their huge communal nests in acacia and quiver trees. African fish eagle, Egyptian goose and pied kingfisher are among other species that frequent the canyon. The pools sustain numbers of blue kurper, carp and yellowfish. Several animals have also made their home in this harsh place – among tracks you may see are those of Burchell's or plains zebra, klipspringer, chacma baboon and rock dassie (or hyrax) but, apart from the bustling insects, lizards and the occasional snake, they are rarely seen.

It is not distance that makes the 86-kilometre (53-mile) long walk along the canyon floor so arduous (and ultimately so satisfying) an experience but the searing, unrelenting daytime heat, and the ruggedness of the terrain. The trail starts, at the main viewpoint ten kilometres (six miles) south of Hobas, with a scramble of at least an hour just to get down to the bottom, and thereafter it's a matter of following the convoluted course of the riverbed. Soft, sandy banks and stretches covered with small round rocks add to your difficulties, and by 11 o'clock in the morning it may be just too hot to continue. A rest in whatever shade you can find is advisable until at least mid-afternoon, when the slanting sun heralds the evening's coolness. Camping sites are where you make them, but a favourite is at the sulphur springs, 16 kilometres (ten miles) from the start, where

The hiking trail, and the canyon proper, end at the springs and resort at Ai-Ais, some 32 kilometres (20 miles) away from the river's confluence with the Orange. Here the softer sedimentary rocks are replaced on the surface by hard-wearing granites, and erosion has been much slower and less dramatic.

Thermal Springs in a Desert

The Nama people called the water Ai-Ais, which means 'scalding', and it seems appropriate that in this sun-blasted canyon even the moisture from the deep ground should be hot, with temperatures hovering around $66°$ Centigrade ($150°$ Fahrenheit). But there is compen-

sation: the water is famed for the healing properties conferred by its high sodium chloride (common salt) and sodium sulphate content and its slight radioactivity.

Ai-Ais, although known for generations, was developed only in the 1960s as a health resort of special benefit to those suffering from rheumatic and arthritic disorders. The Fish River, which has no connection with the spring, provides the water that nourishes the lawns, trees and banks of reeds that surround the resort's airconditioned flats, restaurant and indoor spa.

Getting Around

The canyon lies within the wider Ai-Ais Hot Springs Game Park. The road to its main viewsite and to Ai-Ais is gravel-surfaced, may be quite badly corrugated in parts and, especially on the descent to Ai-Ais, has some impressive hairpin bends. The Fish River Canyon Hiking Trail takes five days to complete. Once you start, there's no turning back. Parties comprise between three and 40 hikers, the most allowed on the trail at any one time.

Staying There

Hobas camp, ten kilometres (six miles) from the start of the Fish River Canyon Hiking Trail, is designed mainly as an overnight stop for parties setting out the next day. Hobas has a caravan and camping ground with ablution and kitchen facilities, a shop and swimming pool. Ai-Ais offers flats, huts, caravan and camping sites, shop, restaurant, swimming pool and tennis courts. Thatched bungalows are available at the privately owned Cañon Lodge.

Above: The brittle-looking milkbush is among a small number of specialized plants that survive the harsh, searingly hot climate of the canyon.

Right: In common with most aloes, the quiver tree will survive in dry, stony places that receive rain only once in two or three years.

NAMIB-NAUKLUFT PARK

The Shifting Sands of a Painted Desert

The park, enormous in extent, hauntingly beautiful in its strangeness, occupies some 50,000 square kilometres (19,000 square miles) of the southern Namib, an ancient desert – it is in fact the world's oldest – that stretches from Swakopmund southwards to the mouth of the Orange River, Namibia's border with South Africa. Its coast, like that to the north, is desolate, the seaboard and hinterland a vast ocean of sand where serried ranks of massive, shifting dunes march to distant horizons.

The dune country is divided from the great gravel plains of the north by the dry bed of the Kuiseb River. About 100 kilometres (60 miles) from the sea, on the eastern boundary of the park, are the Naukluft mountains, source of many ephemeral rivers and of two, the Tsondab and Tsauchab, that have a stronger flow. Even so, they fail to reach the ocean, eventually coming to rest among the sand dunes as pools that serve as havens for the region's scanty but fascinating wildlife.

Opposite, top: The wide spaces of the Namibrand reserve.

Opposite, bottom left: The wedge-snouted desert lizard, an agile creature that dives into the sand to escape an enemy.

Opposite, bottom centre: Pèringuèy's adder, also known as the sidewinding adder for the way it moves across the hot sands.

Opposite, bottom right: The heavily-built Namaqua chameleon.

Top right: The graceful greater flamingo, a familiar sight at Sandwich Harbour.

The Lie of the Land

The northern segment of the park embraces what are known as the Welwitschia Flats. Here the bone-dry Swakop River cuts through flat, gravel plains dotted here and there with rocky outcrops and rows of modest hills. Erosion features called inselbergs, or 'island mountains', rise above a searingly hot, hostile, near barren countryside that, despite its harshness, manages to support a few euphorbias along with the extraordinary welwitschia. The latter, an incredibly hardy plant, lives for 1,500 years and more and in all that time produces just two leaves. These grow continuously, splitting into strips, the outer parts withering beneath the burning sun to produce a tangled mass of vegetation.

To the south of the Flats the plains are cut by the Kuiseb River and other 'watercourses' that, on average, flow only once or twice in a century – and then only sluggishly. But tenacious streams seep beneath the surface, and some of the banks support a light growth of woodland. After rain, carpets of grass appear almost by magic, drawing herds of hungry springbok, gemsbok and zebra.

For most of its length, the Kuiseb runs underground, its course marked by strips of greenery. Once, though, the river flowed strongly, cutting a deep, twisting channel through the soft rocks of the surface. This is Kuiseb Canyon, rugged home to the Topnaar Koina people who, for generations, have dug the ground for water and harvested the earth for the wild nara melon,

Location: West-central Namibia.

Climate: The coast is cool and refreshing all year round; inland temperatures are more extreme. There may be hot winds and sand storms between May and August; nights can be cold throughout the year, sometimes bitterly so.

When to go: At any time, but accommodation is very limited, so book well in advance.

Getting there: For Sandwich Harbour, which is open only to day visitors (with permits), take the 4x4 route south from Walvis Bay. The park's Sesriem Gate is accessible by road from Sandwich Harbour, Walvis Bay, Rehoboth or Maltahöhe. Fly-in safaris are available to almost any destination in the region.

Facilities: Within the park: basic camp sites only; day trails and motor trails, including a two-day 4x4 trail. Luxurious hotel accommodation at Sossusvlei Karos Lodge; guided tours and balloon flights available at Namibrand Nature Reserve.

Wildlife: Where there's water and grass, keep a look out for gemsbok, springbok, zebra and ostrich; bird life is surprisingly brisk and varied. The park's main attractions are its unusual (indeed unique) and incredibly beautiful landscapes.

Permits and reservations: You won't need a permit if you stay on the proclaimed public roads within the park; permits for exploring further afield are available from the Directorate of Tourism (see page 174), and at some filling stations in Swakopmund and Walvis Bay. Accommodation must be booked well in advance.

Precautions: Stock up with water, food, fuel and spares if you intend leaving the public roads.

Above: The wild horses of the Namib are descended from animals imported by the German colonial troops almost a century ago.

Below: Tourists venture into the baking landscape of dunes and skeletal trees near Sossusvlei.

and to shy leopard, baboon, dassie, klipspringer, springbok and the endemic Hartmann's mountain zebra.

Some 70 km (45 miles) south of Walvis Bay, however, the river surfaces in a sandy delta just short of the sea, creating the lonely and bird-haunted wetland known as Sandwich Harbour. The place, though, is no longer a harbour: the relentless march of the dunes has obliterated all signs of human activity (and, it is said, the bones of an 18th-century treasure ship). Sometimes the ocean breaks through the last sand barriers, and the low salinity of the combined waters produces an ecosystem that nurtures dense growths of reeds and grasses and a wealth of aquatic and land birds. Among the annual summer visitors are flamingos and pelicans by the tens of thousands. Despite the depredations of the birds, the lagoon is also a breeding ground for many kinds of fish.

Sand and the Wind

The most fascinating of the Namib's great rows of 'cyclic' or 'parabolic' dunes – product of the sand's looseness and of the winds – are those that are still forming, dissipating, moving on and forming again. In the process they take on different shapes and display the most breathtaking colours, nowhere more so than around Sossusvlei, where variations of light fall onto the tiny quartzite grains and change the hues from maroon to gold to ivory. Some of these dunes reach a height of 385 metres (1,300 feet) – the world's highest.

Sossusvlei is a clay-bedded pan, at the end of the Tsauchab River, where gnarled, 500-year-old camelthorn trees shade a number of attractive picnic sites. The pan is all but surrounded by the glorious freehand curves of the dunes, a unique landscape that is at its most colourfully dramatic around sunrise and sunset, when the fast-changing light works its miracle on the high-piled sand.

On the bone-dry Tsauchab River about 60 kilometres (37 miles) upstream from Sossusvlei is Sesriem ('six-thong') Canyon, a deep and narrow (less than two metres in places) gorge cut into the rock by debris carried down on a younger and more vigorous stream. Its floor is an enchanting oasis, with shade-giving plants and even some large trees growing around pools that attract many species of bird and small animal. The gorge gradually widens until it merges with the flat plain, the river finally disappearing underground at Sossusvlei.

The Living Desert

The Namib's many kinds of lizard, snake and insect are especially fascinating in the way they have adapted to the harshness of desert life. Dunes and plain, in fact, harbour creatures you'll find nowhere else. For example there's the intriguing Peringuey's adder (*Bitis peringueyi*), with eyes at the top of its head – a feature that enables it to lie buried in the sand and still keep watch for approaching prey. Its sideways method of locomotion allows it to move swiftly over loose sand with a minimum of contact with the hot surface. To obtain water, this little snake will often press its body close to the ground at night and let the cold fog condense on its scales. Another unusual dune-dweller is a large spider known as the white lady (*Leucorchestris* sp.), which, when it wants to make a quick exit, simply tucks up its legs and rolls, like a cartwheel, down the side of a dune. Most of the Namib's wildlife species, and especially the insects and other small organisms, are nurtured not by the rain and the ground cover (there is precious little of either) but by the mists that

roll in from the cool Atlantic Ocean, and by breezes that blow from the interior, bringing with them grass segments and other bits of nutritious plant detritus. The occasional pan and natural spring, moreover, sustain a surprising number and variety of larger game, including gemsbok, springbok and Hartmann's mountain zebra, all of which range widely but are most often seen in the grasslands of the east. Along the river courses you'll find steenbok, klipspringer and baboon; black-backed jackal wander freely; among other carnivores are leopard and hyaena of both the brown and the more aggressive spotted kinds.

Getting Around

The road through the Welwitchia Flats is clearly signposted, the boards indicating not only plant life but geological features and places of historic significance as well. A 4x4 is useful but not essential, although you can't get to Sandwich Harbour without one. You'll also have to walk the last four sandy kilometres to Sossusvlei (and back). The 15-kilometre (nine-mile) Tinkas Nature Trail, in the north, is a circular route that takes between four and five hours to complete. There are also delightful walks at Kuiseb, Sesriem Canyon and Sandwich Harbour. The great dunes of Sossusvlei are best explored at sunrise, after which the temperature rises rapidly. The Namib-Naukluft Trail (up to eight days) is open from 1 March to 31 October.

Staying There

There's plenty of good accommodation in Swakopmund and Walvis Bay. For the more adventurous, Kuiseb Canyon offers a basic camping site, but you'll have to take all your equipment. Sandwich Harbour is open to day visitors only. There are also camping sites at Welwitschia, Naukluft and Sesriem, but not at Sossusvlei. Sesriem has a swimming pool and a shop where you can buy wood, fuel and other basic provisions.

Much more comfortable, even luxurious (and superbly designed) is Sossusvlei Karos Lodge, just outside the park, which offers comfortable tented en-suite accommodation, a restaurant, bar and pool.

The extensive Namibrand Nature Reserve, which borders on the Namib-Naukluft, has its headquarters at Wolwedans Dune camp, some 80 kilometres (50 miles) from Sossusvlei. Guests – many of whom arrive on fly-in safaris – enjoy panoramic vistas of varied Namib landscapes, scenic drives, walking trails and the exhilaration of hot-air ballooning.

Above: Faint spoor shows that gemsbok have recently crossed these soaring, shifting sands.

Bottom left: Life-sustaining tsamma melons lie on the desert ground amid a tangle of drying stalks. These plants are closely related to cultivated species of the pumpkin family.

Bottom right: The ragged *Welwitschia mirabilis*, a strange cone-bearing plant, can live for more than 1,500 years in one of the world's most hostile environments.

SKELETON COAST AND HINTERLAND

The Untamed Land

The northern Namibian seaboard is one of the loneliest places on earth, a desolate, other-worldly, ferociously hostile coast of gravel, rock and windswept, drifting sand, of jagged, fog-shrouded reefs and vicious cross-currents that have, over the centuries, claimed the lives of a thousand mariners. Their ships, or what remains of them, litter the shallows and the surfline; most of those men who survived the wrecks perished in the wastes of the hinterland, their bleaching bones, and those of whales and countless seals, giving the region its sinister name.

For all that, though, this remote and rugged maritime strip is a place of revelation: despite its barren bleakness, it has its unearthly beauty – and its fauna and flora, life forms that are remarkable and, some of them, unique in the way they have adapted to the harshness.

Coast and Hinterland

Much of the Namibian coastline, from Oranjemund in the restricted diamond area of the south to the Kunene River in the north, is embraced by national parks and reserves, with the Namib desert running the entire length

Opposite: Desert elephant, believed to be the tallest form of *Loxodonta africana*, share the wide spaces of the Kunene region with the Himba people. Here, a herd passes by one of the lonely settlements.

Top right: The white pelican, renowned for its spectacular flight, has a wingspan of about three metres.

and reaching inland for an average 100 kilometres (60 miles). The northernmost protected area is the Skeleton Coast Park, which extends south from Angola and the Kunene River for 500 kilometres (300 miles) and then, as the National West Coast Tourist Recreation Area, for a further 200 kilometres (125 miles) to the shallow-water harbour of Swakopmund.

The terrain is bone dry; the prevailing wind, which blows off the cold, north-flowing Benguela Current, brings less than 25 millimetres (one inch) of rain in a year. Almost the only source of moisture is the fog that rolls in from the sea each night to deposit a precious film of water on the rocks, the sand and the leaves of the pitifully few plants. The mean annual temperature along the coastal belt remains at the modest 15° Centigrade mark (or 23° Fahrenheit), compared with 21° Centigrade (69° Fahrenheit) on the subcontinent's eastern seaboard.

Inland from the Skeleton Coast lies the Kunene region (until recently known as the Kaokoveld), an untamed and ruggedly beautiful land that rises gently across the great central plains to culminate in a bizarre fantasia of towering heights and deep gorges. Water, while still not plentiful, is at least available at some times and in some places. The landscapes of the Kunene are magnificent, and diverse, encompassing the harsh gravel

Above: Ruppel's parrot, a treetop forager of fruits, seeds and nuts.

Right: The striped tree squirrel is often seen sunning itself on projecting branches.

Below: The Gross Spitzkoppe, a huge 'island' of granite mountains rising from the Namibian plain some 40 kilometres (25 miles) southwest of Usakos.

flats of the desert, sparsely covered grassland, dusty mopane scrub and the many-hued mountain ranges of the east. Only close to the Kunene River and along the mostly dry, westward flowing 'watercourses' is the land wrapped in greenery.

The Kunene region, one of the wildest, least disturbed parts of the world, can nevertheless be explored in reasonable safety, even comfort, providing one prepares well for the journey. A grand tour will take in, among much else, the immense series of massifs known as the Brandberg and its thousands of ancient rock paintings (these are ranked among the finest examples of Bushman art, and include the famed and controversial 'White Lady'); the vast and starkly eroded Gross Spitzkoppe (whose summit was first scaled only in 1947); the Twyfelfontein moonscape, its jumbled outcrops and elaborate rock engravings (thought to be the work of ancestral Khoi; the later paintings are Bushman in origin); the petrified forest at Khorixas; and the flat-topped mountains and cone-shaped hills beyond Etendeka.

Desert Wildlife

The coastal strip supports practically no vegetation, though a little way inland you'll find scatters of hardy plants in the dry riverbeds, and succulents, ever-lastings (Compositae) and the occasional stunted acacia elsewhere. There is also the welwitschia, an untidy straggle of leaf which is actually a dwarf form of tree and which the great Charles Darwin described as 'the platypus of the Plant Kingdom'. Some specimens of this tenaciously drought resistant plant are more than 1,500 years old (see also page 115).

Splashes of white and orange on the rocks are plaques of lichens, the product of a symbiotic relationship between algae and fungi. Fog and sunlight provide just

Left: Cape fur seals are superb swimmers, though they spend about a third of their lives, including their breeding season, on firm ground. Males are fiercely territorial.

Below: A bull elephant, well adapted to the desert spaces, stretches to reach the most tender branches of an ana tree.

the right balance to make the Skeleton Coast, with more than 100 species, one of the richest and most fascinating lichen grounds in the world.

Life in the region, however, is by no means confined to plants. A surprising variety of birds, lizards, snakes, arachnids and insects inhabit the hostile countryside. Mammals too: remarkably, the most visible of the coastal creatures is the black-backed jackal. This resourceful animal scavenges the beaches and, quite unafraid, slinks and hovers around anglers, patiently waiting for the offal to be thrown aside when the catch is cleaned. The brown hyaena has also taken to life along the tide-line, but tends to emerge only at night. The jackal on the other hand may be seen almost any time – and in fair numbers at Cape Cross, where, in the summer breeding season, there are some quarter of a million Cape fur seals in residence. Among the area's seabirds are innumerable cormorants, which roost at the Cape, making daily journeys to and from their feeding grounds.

On the forbidding inland plains are gemsbok, springbok, ostrich, black rhino, giraffe, Hartmann's mountain zebra, leopard – and the famed desert elephant. These huge mammals, along with black rhino, are sometimes seen only a few kilometres from the beaches as they range widely (up to 70 kilometres/45 miles each day) in their quest for food and water. Elephant are normally – elsewhere – incredibly destructive, casually pushing over and destroying a tree simply to get to the tender shoots in the topmost branches, but these desert animals are sensible feeders, careful to conserve their scanty resources. Most

have small tusks, the growth of their ivory inhibited by mineral deficiencies. The population has been declining and now stands at a little less than 100 head.

People of the Region

The plains are also home to the Tjima and the Ovahimba, highly distinctive sub-groups of the much more numerous Herero people.

The Ovahimba are semi-nomadic pastoralist folk who have clung tenaciously to their traditional ways, shunning most of the trappings of 'civilization' in their (so far) successful bid to keep their cultural heritage intact. They subsist on the milk of their goats and cattle and on the hardy plants of an ungenerous land, and still wear their softly tanned leather skirts, beads and tubular bracelets, with sometimes a cowrie shell or whelk (a marine mollusc) slung around the neck. They have adopted a few modern comforts, such as blankets and buckets, but generally live very much in the way of their forbears.

Getting Around

Although the region does have its wildlife, its attractions lie mostly in its vast landscapes, and its solitude, and in the spiritual experience these confer. A four-wheel-drive vehicle is recommended. The Ugab River Hiking Trail, the Skeleton Coast Park's only trail, is a 50-kilometre (30-mile) circular route that takes three days to complete.

Hikers bring their own food and equipment, and must have a medical certificate of fitness. Inland is the Brandberg, a towering island of granite (its highest point, Konigstein, rises 2,573 metres/8,440 feet above sea level) whose several thousand prehistoric rock paintings can be viewed along a short trail, a popular walk that starts from the parking area and proceeds along a shady ravine. The petrified forest near Khorixas is also worth seeing: it consists of tumbled, long fossilized tree trunks that are almost 300 million years old, and, like Twyfelfontein (see above, page 118), is signposted from the road to the coast.

Staying There

Khorixas is an ideal inland base from which to explore the Kunene region and offers a range of accommodation. Terrace Bay, on the coast, has bungalows with full board. There are camping and caravan sites at Torra Bay, well provided with fresh water, firewood and other facilities, but the place is open only during the months of December and January. Etendeka has an airstrip, and can be reached – except for the last few kilometres – by ordinary saloon car (the proprietors provide a 4x4 pickup service over the final stretch).

Among the more remote and enticing of the region's private lodges is Palmwag (an attractive and resfreshingly comfortable base from which Desert Adventure Safaris operates); the two-star Otjiwa Game Ranch, and Otjisazu Hunting and Guest Farm. Farther inland and not strictly part of the region, but still conveniently located, are the Okapuka Lodge and the luxurious, game-rich Mount Etjo Safari Lodge, some 25 kilometres (15 miles) to the north of Windhoek.

ETOSHA NATIONAL PARK

The Waters of Life

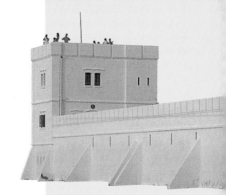

Etosha Pan – the 'place of dry water' or the 'big dry place' – is an enormous, shallow depression of some 5,000 square kilometres (2,000 square miles) scraped out of an otherwise semi arid plain. It is a desolate and intimidating corner of Africa, a vast, flat, sun-baked 'salt desert' of hard, deeply cracked clay whose harsh whiteness dazzles the eye and deceives the mind with mirages that shimmer in the rising heat. The earth here is barren – but it is not always dry: occasionally, for a few months, distant rains are channelled in to fill the pan with a few centimetres of water and this, together with the run-off from two perennial, mineral-rich springs, is enough to sustain a marvellous profusion of living forms.

According to legend, the pan – 130 kilometres (80 miles) at its longest, 50 kilometres (30 miles) at its widest – was created by the tears of a young woman who had seen her family killed by warlike strangers. Geologists, however, have another, less romantic expla-

Opposite, top: Burchell's zebra drink their fill at one of the many natural springs near the edge of Etosha Pan.

Opposite, bottom left: A herd of eland, ever conscious of predators, makes its cautious way to a waterhole.

Opposite, bottom right: The shy and dainty Damara dik-dik is notable for its elongated, trunk-like muzzle.

Top right: The old fort at Namutoni, a romantic looking structure built by the German colonists for defence and now part of the park's visitor accommodation.

nation – that the depression was once a vast lake, fed by rivers that have either long since dried up or which were forced, by movements of the earth, to change course.

The bed of the pan is too salty to support vegetation, but the surrounding countryside – the wider park covers more than 20,000 square kilometres (7,500 square miles) – is mostly open grassland with tracts of scrubby bush and semi-deciduous woodland of mopane and acacia. For a brief while, however, much of the region's life is centred on the great expanse of shallow water, the pan itself.

Until the rains begin, Etosha's animals must drink at watering points which dwindle in number with the winter drought – and during these months there are easy pickings for lions and other predators. Happily, though, the carnivore and herbivore populations are in equilibrium, and the park is able to sustain these natural mortalities.

Lions are the chief but by no means only predators: cheetah, leopard, hyaena, black-backed jackal and several kinds of smaller cat also hunt on the broad, sandy, heat-hazed plains. Prominent grazers and browsers among the park's 144 mammal species are elephant (up to 2,500 of them at times), zebra, wildebeest, giraffe, gemsbok, kudu, springbok, the rare black-faced impala – and black rhino, perhaps the most threatened of all Africa's larger animals.

During the early 1970s the continent's black rhino population, although already suffering from indiscriminate hunting, stood at 65,000. Then, in little more than

Location: Northern Namibia, 450 km (280 miles) north of Windhoek.

Climate: Etosha lies within the tropics; the weather is generally hot, especially from October to April. Night temperatures may drop to below freezing in winter.

When to go: August and September are the best months for viewing Etosha's wildlife.

Getting there: Drive from Windhoek to Otjiwarongo on the B1 national highway. For Namutoni, continue on the B1 via Tsumeb. For Okaukuejo, take the C38 from Otjiwarongo via Outjo. There are three airstrips in the park; others at the private lodges just outside the park.

Facilities: Three rest camps with chalets, caravan parks, 'tourisettes', and Fort Namutoni itself, provide accommodation; restaurant, shop, pool at each camp; picnic sites; network of good gravel roads; basic car repairs at Okaukuejo.

Equipment: Take your own cooking utensils, crockery and cutlery. Carry water and emergency rations in case of mechanical breakdown, and check that your spare wheel is inflated and in good condition.

Wildlife: Elephant, giraffe, black and white rhino, plains zebra, wildebeest, kudu, eland, gemsbok, hartebeest, the rare black-faced impala and other antelope species; lion, leopard, cheetah, spotted and brown hyaena (more than 140 mammal species altogether); plus some 340 species of bird.

Permits and reservations: Entrance fees are payable at Namutoni and Okaukuejo. Book your accommodation well in advance (see page 174).

Precautions: The Etosha park is a low-risk malaria area.

two decades, it plunged to a pitiful 2,500, with most of the survivors resident in South Africa and Namibia. Rhino protection campaigns had been launched in both countries in mid-1960s. In Namibia the animals were moved from the more accessible areas – those surrounded by farmland – to Etosha, where vigilant wardens and the vast, inhospitable spaces watched over them. The park is now home for around 300 black rhino of the local endemic subspecies while Namibia, as a whole, hosts the largest free-roaming rhino population in the world. Moreover the situation is healthy enough, and the future secure enough, for Namibian black rhinos to have been translocated to other southern African conservation areas.

Antelope are well represented, ranging in size from the tiny 5-kilogram (11-pound), shy Damara dik-dik to the kudu and gemsbok, both of which tip the scales at around 240 kilograms (530 pounds) or more. The gems-bok, with its tapering, sword-like horns forming a V atop its handsome head, is a powerful and elegant inhabitant of some of the hottest spots on earth, yet it rarely drinks: the animal obtains most of its moisture from wild melons, and by digging up succulent roots and bulbs. It maintains an unusually high body temperature (its brain is kept cool by an ingenious mechanism, located within the nasal cavity, known as the carotid rete) and rarely perspires, so conserving water. The territorial leader of a gemsbok herd marks his patch with piles of dung pellets, and will put up an intimidating display, pawing the earth and thrusting with his horns, to discourage other males.

Wings Across the Desert

As the pan fills, greater and lesser flamingos in their thousands home in, looking for the hummocks that rise above the water and on which they can raise their broods in safety. Theirs is a frantic race against time: their young must learn to fly before the waters evaporate and the predators move in. When the adults can delay no longer, they depart, leaving to their fate those chicks that are still earthbound. The chicks then set off on a desperate walk to safety, but few survive.

Above: A handsomely coloured Egyptian goose puts on a menacing 'threat' display to warn intruders away from its territory.

Below: Small clumps of reed-like grasses provide a surprising amount of cover, even for an animal as large as this young lion.

Getting Around

The main game-viewing road network skirts the southern shore of the pan, running northeast for 135 kilometres (84 miles) from Okaukuejo (Andersson Gate) to Namutoni (Von Lindequist Gate). Minor roads weave away from the route, leading to some 30 spring-fed waterholes. Like predators in the dry season, one has only to wait patiently – preferably parked in the shade – to be sure of a good day's viewing. Park staff say that concentrating on one promising waterhole usually produces better results than chasing from place to place. Each camp has a floodlit waterhole, conveniently sited for both the wildlife and its observers. The animals have become accustomed to the floodlighting and to the human presence. Access to the western section, via Galton Gate at Otjovasondu, is reserved for registered

Left: The endangered black rhino is extinct throughout much of its former range; in Namibia, by happy contrast, its numbers are growing, albeit slowly.

Overleaf: An elephant herd advances with single minded purpose towards an Etosha waterhole.

Below: Although the giraffe can go for long periods without drinking, it will regularly slake its thirst when water is available. It is most vulnerable to predators when bending down, awkwardly, to take its fill.

Pelicans, red-billed teal, stork, ibis and egret are among other waterbirds that travel long distances to reach Etosha. Also seen are the bright hues of the crimson-breasted shrike, Namibia's national bird, and the beautiful lilac-breasted roller. Altogether, the park sustains well over 300 kinds of bird ranging from the giant ostrich down to the tiny prinias.

Right: Drinking is a luxury for the powerfully built and elegant gemsbok, which obtains most of its moisture from melons, and from the bulbs and roots it digs up.

Below: Greater flamingos, invariably seen in large flocks, feed only on the tiny aquatic organisms that they filter through a special structure in their bills. Their bills are pink with a black tip; the lesser flamingo's bill is a dark red colour.

tour operators. Roads are gravel-surfaced and well maintained, but punctures are a common occurrence (camp staff will mend these for you). Fuel is readily available at all three camps.

A private tour operator supplies vehicles to visitors who arrive by air: there are airstrips at the three internal camps and also at the private lodges situated just outside the park.

There's an information centre and a watch-tower, built in the early German colonial days, at Okaukuejo. The museum in Namutoni's lookout tower graphically recounts the fort's history. A shady, thatched platform overlooks Namutoni's waterhole.

Staying There

The three rest camps in the park are Namutoni in the east, Okaukuejo in the south, and Halali, about midway between the two. Namutoni is rather special: it started life (in 1905) as a German colonial fort – reputedly the most handsome in all of Germany's overseas possessions – and the building, a romantically picturesque *Beau Geste*-type affair, has changed

little in the more than 90 years since. It now forms the striking centrepiece of the rest camp. Each place offers the welcome luxury of a swimming pool, a restaurant and accommodation ranging from caravan and camping sites to very comfortable bungalows and rondavels. Guests at Namutoni have the option of sleeping in the historic fort.

Well-appointed private lodges on or beyond the perimeter serve as ideal bases from which to explore Etosha in the company of an experienced game guide. Mokuti Lodge, close to Von Lindequist Gate, offers guided hikes through the bush country that surrounds the park (visitors are not allowed to walk within its bounds, mainly because of the lions). The western section of the park is accessible only by special arrangement, but Hobatere Lodge, near Galton Gate, lays on hikes, day and night drives, and scenic flights by light aircraft. Ongava, a private game reserve and lodge some seven kilometres (4 ½ miles) from Andersson Gate, is a sanctuary for white rhino and for some rare antelope species, including the black-faced impala and the roan.

Left: The historic watch-tower at Okaukuejo, head-quarters of the Etosha National Park.

THE CAPRIVI REGION

Fertile Floodplains of the North

The Caprivi region or 'strip' is a tongue of land, measuring some 450 kilometre (280 miles) from west to east and no more than 80 kilometres (50 miles) wide, that juts out from the northeast corner of Namibia. Here flow the bountiful waters of the Kavango (or Okvango), the Kwando, the Linyanti (known as the Chobe in its lower reaches), the mighty Zambezi and other rivers, watercourses that serve as major thoroughfares. River-craft range from the stately, three-decked *Zambezi Queen* to the traditional *mokoro* or dug-out canoe. Four countries – Namibia, Botswana, Zambia and Zimbabwe – meet at Caprivi's eastern tip. The rivers and their floods are the very lifeblood of the region's wild animals and its people, nurturing the land, yielding their bounty to the fisher-folk, sustaining the herders and their cattle.

Caprivi's Havens

Mahango Game Reserve, situated on the wide, lush plains of the Kavango River at the western end of Caprivi, is a magical expanse of wetland, woodland and

Opposite, top: Sundown on the Chobe River, known as the Linyanti in its western reaches and one of Caprivi's major watercourses. The region enjoys only moderate rainfall, but seasonal floods inundate the countryside around.

Opposite, bottom: Cattle egrets are popularly known as 'tick birds' from the way they cling to the hides of both domestic stock and the larger game animals, where they feed on the parasites. This one rests atop a hippo's head.

Top right: One of the frog species found on the Linyanti River, a major watercourse of the Caprivi region.

riverine forest open only to day visitors. Just 15 kilometres (nine miles) north of its entrance, though – and an excellent base from which to explore the area – is the river-bank Popa Falls rest camp. The falls themselves are more a series of swirling rapids than the classic tumbling cataract, but in their own way they are no less impressive. Adjoining the reserve is the Caprivi Game Park, which is similar in its terrain, fauna and flora but larger – 570 square kilometres (220 square miles) in extent – and rather more accessible (a good road bisects it from east to west).

In East Caprivi, across the Kwando River and extending along its left bank, lies the Mudumu National Park, a 1,100-square kilometre (390-square mile) swathe of savanna and woodland gradually merging with the swamps and plains of adjoining Mamili National Park. Mamili's wetlands – the Linyanti swamps – are a blend of floodplains, reedbeds and small lakes dotted with flowering lilies, all cut through by lazily meandering waterways. Both Mamili and Mudumu, which were proclaimed in 1990, boast a quite remarkable diversity of game. Especially prolific and varied are the area's birds – no fewer than 400 species have been recorded, many of them waterbirds. Some, like the wattled crane, swamp boubou, slaty egret and lesser jacana, have a very limited distribution.

Islands in a Stream

When the floods come, in June, close to 80 per cent of Mamili is inundated by the Kwando and Linyanti rivers, with just a few higher-lying hillocks protruding as

---

Location: Caprivi is a narrow panhandle jutting eastwards from Namibia's northeastern corner.

Climate: Winter days are mild to warm; winter nights can be chilly. Summers are very hot.

When to go: Conditions for game viewing are usually at their best from August through to October.

Getting there: The main highway leads through Windhoek, bearing northeast through Grootfontein and Rundu to Caprivi. Road access from South Africa is shorter, the route running through Botswana, via Francistown, Nata and Kasane. There are scheduled flights to Katima Mulilo.

Facilities: Guided walks and game-drives; riverboat rides offer game-watching from the water.

Activities: One hires a *mokoro* (dugout canoe) for fishing, bird-spotting, game-watching or just cruising gently on the river.

Wildlife: Caprivi is home to elephant, hippo, crocodile, lion, buffalo, leopard, cheetah, and many antelope species including a number rarely seen elsewhere. Visibility may be somewhat restricted in the well-treed areas. The region also sustains a huge variety of bird life.

Permits and reservations: Permits are required for entry into Mamili, Mudumu and Mahango. Book in advance for the Popa Falls rest camp. Contact the Namibian Ministry of Wildlife, Conservation and Tourism (see page 174).

Precautions: Take precautions against malaria (this is a high-risk area), especially during the summer months. Water from taps is usually purified, but you'll need to treat the water in the remoter parts. Crocodiles and hippo can be dangerous. Be alert; don't swim until you know it's quite safe to do so.

luxuriantly vegetated islands. The largest of these, Nkasa and Lupala, are well worth a special visit for their magnificent birds and varied plant life. So too is strategically positioned Impalila Island, at the confluence of the Zambezi and Chobe rivers – the point where the borders of four countries (see above, p.131) come together. Visitors to baobab-shaded Impalila Island Lodge explore the waterways by *mokoro*, or go game-watching by boat along the Chobe River. Impalila is noted for the tigerfishing in its surrounding waters and, most notably, for the variety of its bird species.

Zambezi Lodge, near Katima Mulilo (the region's administrative centre) serves as home port to the *Zambezi Queen* river-boat, perhaps the most elegant and comfortable game-viewing platform you'll find anywhere. It has two lounges, a cocktail bar, entertainment deck, dining room and airconditioned cabins.

Many of the indigenous people of Caprivi are related to the Barotse (or Lozi) of southwestern Zambia; others – those farther west – are thought to descend from the Bushman and other Khoina peoples of the South Africa's Cape regions. The Caprivi Art Centre in Katimo Mulilo displays their distinctive craftwork, including pottery, wood-carvings and basketry.

The Big Four – and More

Caprivi's wildlife is both varied and, for the most part, highly visible. Crocodile have been recorded, and at least 60 species of mammal, including the hippo and four of the 'big five' – elephant, buffalo, lion and leopard. Most of the animals are found throughout the region, though some favour a particular environment or locality. Caprivi is also sanctuary for one of Africa's rarest antelopes, the water-adapted sitatunga, which haunts the papyrus swamps that are its home and refuge. The animal is a powerful swimmer and, equipped with remarkably elongated, pointed hooves, runs easily and silently over the soft, swampy surfaces. It can sometimes be seen on hard ground, but here it moves clumsily and far prefers the friendlier water and its papyrus and reed beds. Caprivi's rivers and streams are well stocked with tigerfish, a fine game species that attracts angling enthusiasts from afar.

Getting Around

The main road that runs across Caprivi to Katima Mulilo and beyond into Botswana (as mentioned, it actually passes through Caprivi Game Park) is negotiable by the ordinary family saloon car, as is the road to the private lodge at Lianshulu, within Mudumu National Park. So too is one of Mahango's roads, a route that leads past two picnic sites and traverses part of the floodplain. Popa Falls rest camp is also readily accessible, but, for the rest, visitors to Caprivi will need a 4x4 vehicle and a spirit of adventure.

Staying There

Lianshulu, a private lodge within Mudumu National Park, has an airstrip and offers guided nature drives, walks, boat trips and a sunset cruise. Mvubu Lodge, also within Mudumu, is set on an oxbow lake in the backwaters of the Kwando River and comprises two-person tents encircling a central complex of restaurant, bar and outdoor eating area.

Mamili National Park embraces the shady Impalila Island Lodge (see opposite page). Downstream at Katima Mulilo there's the Zambezi Lodge, which despite its name is a comfortable, even luxurious hotel with a restaurant, floating bar, pool, gymnasium and golf course. There are no rest camps actually within the Mahango Game Reserve, but close to the entrance gate is the Popa Falls rest camp (self-catering accommoda-tion) and the privately run Suclabo venue, an attractively rustic cluster of comfortable huts and tents.

The riverside chalets of Kalizo Fishing Lodge are on the Zambezi some 40 kilometres (25 miles) downstream of Katima Mulilo. Kalizo provides excellent fishing throughout the year; in January, it is entirely surrounded by water and guests are boated to their angling spots.

Above: Subiya fishermen on the Linyanti River prepare to cast their nets.

Below: Graceful white pelicans spread their three-metre wingspan as they drop in among a flock of sacred ibis.

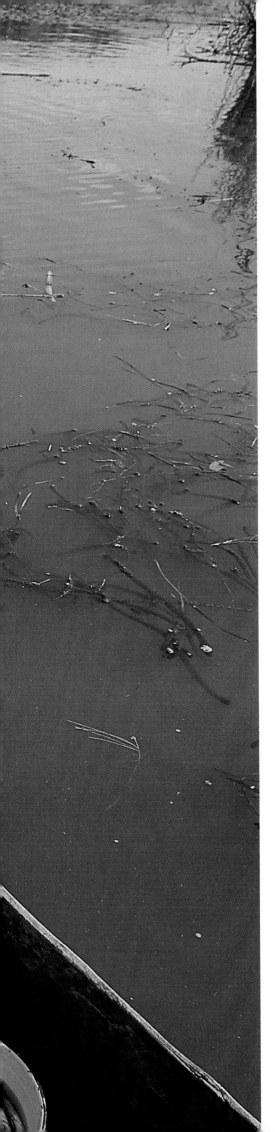

BOTSWANA

Botswana is a vast, landlocked, sparsely populated country extending across nearly 600,000 square kilometres (230,000 square miles) of flattish countryside that consists, for the most part, of hot Kalahari sand. The land, part of a vast depression scraped out of southern Africa's great interior plateau, receives only modest and unpredictable amounts of rain and is blessed with very little surface water, but, still, only the red dunelands of the far south corresponds to one's perception of a 'true' desert.

The main centres, among them Gaberone, the attractive little national capital, are concentrated along the line of rail that fringes the eastern border; most of the remainder of the country – the endless and often featureless central and western plains – are covered by scanty but sweet grasses that sustain huge herds of cattle, and by scrub and the occasional stand of hardy acacia. Quite different in character is Botswana's far northwest corner. Here water is usually abundant and, some of it, permanent as well, the terrain surprisingly lush in appearance. This is the area nurtured by the Okavango River, which rises in the uplands of neighbouring Angola and makes its way, not to the sea but southeastwards, across Namibia's Caprivi region, to fan out and die in the porous sands of the interior.

For all its great, arid spaces and apparent emptiness, Botswana plays host to some of the highest concentrations of plains big game in Africa. Especially well endowed are the Chobe park, part of which flanks the northern river system, and the splendid Moremi reserve that encroaches onto the Okavango wetlands.

Official policy favours low-volume, relative highly priced tourism, which works to restrict the disruptive human presence and thus helps conserve the fragile environment. Amenities within Botswana's national parks tend to be minimal. The private safari companies, however, offer plenty of other options in terms of both sightseeing and accommodation – the hotels, lodges and camps are invariably well appointed, some of them falling into the luxury category. Most roads in the remoter areas are best suited to four-wheel-drive vehicles, and visitors are advised to travel in convoy in case of accident or breakdown.

Left: Young children of Botswana's wetlands take home the river's bounty. Some of the fish will be eaten fresh; much will be dried for later use.

Above: Hippo spend most of their days partially submerged, their nights grazing.

OKAVANGO AND MOREMI

The Great Inland Delta

Nearly all of land-locked Botswana is taken up by a vast, semiarid plain of Kalahari sand that supports sparse grasslands. The country has almost no surface water, and even underground water is scarce. In the far northwest, however, the Okavango River, deflected east to the interior instead of west to the sea, flows down from the highlands of Angola and, after crossing the border between Botswana and Namibia's Caprivi (see page 131), divides into an expanding network of channels, lagoons and islands, reedbeds and shallows that, together, comprise one of world's last great wetland wildernesses.

At flood time, the delta sprawls out across almost 15,000 square kilometres (580 square miles) in a broad, shallow, fan-shaped basin that hosts a huge number and variety of life forms. The floods begin with the November rains in Angola, and the river rises gently to a peak around February or March, the distant, low-lying floodplains continuing to fill until the wetlands reach their most southerly limit – near the lively little town of

Opposite: The Okavango River winds its way though dense riverine vegetation before fanning out into its immense delta.

Top right: Delicately tinted water lilies grace many of the delta's channels and lagoons.

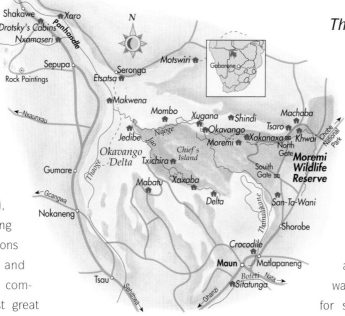

Maun – in May or June. In years of exceptional rainfall, there may even be enough water to flow south into Lake Ngami. For most of the time, however, this mysterious lake, which came and went according to the generosity of the seasons and which so fascinated Victorian explorers, now remains a dry and dusty plain.

The Panhandle

At its point of entry into Botswana, at the country's far northwest corner, the Okavango River flows through a main channel on the relatively narrow floodplain called the Panhandle. Clear and deep, the perennial waters run fairly swiftly for some 100 kilometres (60 miles) through dense growths of papyrus, its banks enlivened by fishing and farming villages of mud and reed homes. Here the islands, so substantial and numerous downstream, are little more than termite heaps, many of them sporting growth of just a single palm tree.

Visitor activities in the Panhandle are centred on water rather than game. The area is known for the splendid opportunities it offers for boating, fishing – especially for the fighting tigerfish – and birding. More than 500 avian species have been recorded in the wider delta area, including that perennial favourite, the African fish eagle. This striking-looking raptor's high, ringing call, the quintessential sound of wild Africa, is most often heard

Location: Northwestern Botswana.

Climate: Winters are dry, most rain falling between December and February. Winter nights and early mornings may be bitterly cold; unpleasantly strong winds blow in August and September; summer days are hot.

When to go: Game concentrates from August to November but a late visit may be spoilt by early rain. Many of the lodges close between December and February.

Getting there: Most visitors arrive in the delta region by air and complete the journey to their camp or lodge by 4x4 or by boat – and sometimes by both.

Facilities: Wide range of accommodation with many lodges offering swimming pools, bars, restaurants, guided safaris. Fishing tackle, canoes and boats may be hired.

Wildlife: Most large mammals are present: sable, sitatunga and roan are the rare species; lechwe, though rare elsewhere, are abundant; hippo and crocodile are prominent in the waterways. One of the largest surviving wild dog populations in Africa ranges near Mombo Camp. The bird list is impressive.

Landscapes: Lazy waterways and lagoons; placid lakes girded by luxuriant vegetation; forest, woodland, floodplain and grassland.

Permits and reservations: No permits are required for entry into the delta area. The fee for entry to Moremi is paid on arrival, but accommodation should be reserved in advance. This is most conveniently done as part of the service offered by safari operators.

Precautions: Malaria; water hazards include crocodiles, hippo and the bilharzia worm.

silent and unobtrusive, is the ideal vehicle for getting around the waterways. Hippo and crocodile pose a risk to tourists intent on poling their own way across the waters, but local people are willing enough to act (for a fee) as boatmen and guides.

Although more than half of Botswana's people (collectively known as Batswana) are Tswana, related to the Sotho of Lesotho and South Africa, the folk of the waterways mostly belong to the Bayei or Hambukushu groups. The ancestors of the Bayei – refugees from oppression – arrived from Zambia in the late 18th century and tended to settle near the shallower reaches, living off and trading with the fish they caught in their reed traps and woven baskets. The Hambukushu on the other hand, although known as deep-water people who, like the Bayei, used the *mokoro* (but paddled rather than poled), were agriculturalists as well as fishers, and their fishing technique – they used nets in the deeper channels – differed from that of their Bayei neighbours. Modern escapees from more troubled regions, and especially from war-torn Angola, are also part of the delta's human tapestry. Many of the villagers wear customary dress at weddings and on other ceremonial occasions – long leather skirts and trailing wigs of sisal, all adorned with beads, copper and brass.

Above: An expertly poled *mokoro* is the ideal vehicle for exploring the wetlands.

Right: A Hambukushu girl displays the family's reed fishing baskets.

Below: Villagers of the delta paddle their way over the waters in the way of their forefathers.

in the early morning and in the evening as it makes its long, shallow glide over the water to rise again with a squirming fish in its talons.

Game viewing in the Panhandle can be difficult because the area sustains, apart from crocodile, hippo and water leguaan (the giant monitor lizard), comparatively few of the larger species, and those that are present, like the sitatunga and lechwe, tend to be shy. Moreover, the dense vegetation, which adds so much to the ambience of the area, to the air of remoteness and restfulness it imparts, restricts one's range of vision. Villagers do much of their travelling by *mokoro* (plural: *mekoro*), the traditional dugout canoe which, being fast,

A guided boat trip by night, with a spotlight, is a memorable experience that will often reveal more than you'll see by daylight: blue-cheeked bee-eaters and kingfishers fast asleep, for example, or night herons and Pel's fishing owls on the hunt. Even the sitatunga antelope, elusive by day, can be observed out in the open during the dark hours.

The Panhandle's main centre is Shakawe, a largish village and resort popular for the bird-spotting and fishing opportunities it provides. From here, too, you can organise a day trip to Tsodilo Hills, outcrops that rise some 400 metres (1,300 feet) above the Kalahari sands and whose rocks, overhangs and caverns serve as canvasses for around 2,500 ancient Bushman (or San) paintings.

Visitors to the Panhandle have a choice of several private camps and lodges, comfortable and for the most part exceptionally attractive little venues. They include Drotsky's Cabins (which offers chalets and reed huts), Xaro Lodge (luxurious tents), Nxamaseri Lodge (chalets) and Shakawe Fishing Camp (tents and brick-under-thatch units).

The Wider Wetlands

The great inland delta fans out from the bottom of the Okavango River's 'stem' (the Panhandle) in an intricate fantasia of channels, lagoons and lakes, the waterways radiating across the grassy and wooded floodplains to create a region of permanent water. Beyond this is the outer fringe, where the dwindling flow forms pans among sandy ridges that support low, scrubby vegetation with occasional patches of taller acacia. Both the delta's inner (or, more correctly, lower) and outer regions are havens for wildlife which, if no longer present in the immense numbers claimed by early travellers, is still represented by a fine diversity in a setting of unspoilt beauty.

As the main stream divides into its increasing number of gradually diminishing watercourses, so it creates a luxuriant and colourful environment that embraces upwards of a thousand islands, some many kilometres across, others just a few square metres in extent. Among and around them the water forms a myriad winding channels and the occasional largish lake, their flows so languid that they carry almost no visible suspended matter, and the water remains remarkably clear, even where reeds grow thickly.

Left: The ringing cry of the African fish eagle is a familiar, and evocative, sound of the wetlands.

Below: Hippos in the Moremi reserve. These bulky, semi-aquatic mammals usually graze at night.

Above: Some of Moremi's elephants. Despite their bulk, these giants can cover the ground at a surprisingly fast speed.

Right: A lioness carries her two-month old cub to safety in gentle jaws.

Below: The warthog goes to ground tail first, its formidable tusks discouraging attack from the rear.

In the more open stretches, the large and almost circular leaf-pads of water lilies lie on the still surface, their delicately tinted flower heads raised. The most widely distributed of these plants is the day lily, which produces flowers varying in colour from blue and purple to rose pink and white.

Beneath the surface are, among other species, tigerfish, bream and barbel (catfish). Angling is at its best from September (August in the Panhandle) through to February; tackle may be hired locally, and you'll need a permit only if you intend to fish within a proclaimed game reserve (most of the delta region has not been so proclaimed). The annual 'barbel run' starts in September, when the fish leave their shallow and drying side-streams to gather in the larger channels and lakes. The dense shoals, preying on the smaller species, attract hosts of birds that include kingfisher, stork, darter and cormorant. Crocodiles join in this moving feast as it makes its spectacular way upstream.

The Delta's Trees

Trees of the acacia family, although more familiar to us as drought-resistant species, are also prominent in the wetlands, especially umbrella thorn, knobthorn, camelthorn and blackthorn, the latter two producing seed pods that are savoured by many game species.

Another member of the family, the water acacia, frequently forms shrub-like thickets and displays flowers of bright golden-yellow balls in August and September. Elsewhere, notably in drier environments, the water aca-

cia is known to be a signpost to underground water. Then there's the sausage tree, remarkable for its large, sausage-shaped fruit, which ripens between December and June and may weigh as much as ten kilograms (22 pounds). Although not particularly tasty or nutritious, the fruit is traditionally used for medicinal purposes. It is also hung in homes as a charm against whirlwinds. Palms, especially of the Phoenix and Hyphaene (fan palm) families, also flourish, lending an air of tropical abundance to the region.

The Bigger Animals

The most numerous of the delta's larger life-forms are buffalo, which are sometimes seen in combined herds of up to a thousand individuals. Groups of other grazers, among them impala, eland, kudu and wildebeest and rather smaller numbers of the handsome sable, range between the lower and outer areas of the delta, while the water-adapted sitatunga and lechwe are found only in the wetlands. Both these species have evolved long, splayed hooves that enable them to move swiftly over the soft surfaces, and both are powerful swimmers.

Predators include lion, leopard, cheetah and wild dog, the last-named among the most endangered of Africa's mammals. Wild dogs hunt in nomadic, restless

packs – demonstrating a single-minded and ferocious display of teamwork – in the early morning or evening. When they've made their kill, they allow the young first fill of the carcass which, in the wild kingdom, is unusual behaviour indeed.

Birds of the Wetlands

The delta's bird life is at its busiest in summer (between October and February), and is especially animated in the Panhandle area and the Moremi Wildlife Reserve in the northeast. Patience, skill – and luck – will reward the bird-spotter handsomely.

An especially intriguing species is the black egret, which adopts a position known as canopying, opening its wings above its head rather like an umbrella, most probably to exclude reflection from the water while peering beneath the surface for its prey. A group of black egrets performing the manoeuvre in unison is particularly impressive. A rare relative is the slaty egret, which, despite many similarities, never canopies.

Moremi Wildlife Reserve

The Moremi sanctuary occupies the northeastern part of the delta, its 1,800-square kilometres (700 square miles) of pristine Africa a lasting tribute to its founders. In the 1950s the local Tswana people whose home it was, feared for the future as more and more hunters arrived to take savage toll of their precious game resources – and they moved, voluntarily, to make room for a formally protected area. The reserve was named after their late leader, Moremi III. He is also recalled in

Chief's Island, a huge (100 X 15 kms (60 X 90 miles)) expanse of grassland and forest occupying about a third of the reserve. The island, flanked by two of the region's largest streams – the Boro and the Santantadibe – is true wilderness: there are strict controls on human habitation and access. The tented Mombo Camp, near the island's northern tip, is famous for the packs of wild dogs that frequent the area. Elephant, giraffe, buffalo, tsessebe, kudu, warthog and scrambling troops of baboons are readily seen, and the bird life is both colourful and prolific.

Below: Burchell's or plains zebra splash their way across a pan in the game-rich Moremi reserve.

Above: A communal river-bank nest can house as many as 5,000 carmine bee-eaters.

Below: Among the stranger residents of the wetlands is the hamerkop, which emits an eerie cry and is known, among some African communities, as the 'bird of doom'.

Motor vehicles are not permitted on Chief's Island. Indeed, much of the wider Moremi area is inaccessible by car (though there are roads in the eastern section), and most visitors arrive by light aircraft.

Moremi is large enough to encompass the full range of Okavango habitats. It also includes the spacious expanse of Xakanaxa Lagoon, an area which, with its four lodges and a camping site, game-viewing and water activities, offers much as a tourist destination. Moreover, much of the reserve lies above the level of the flood-plains and does not become inundated, a feature that attracts many large grazers. The mopane woodlands of the east, for instance, play host to great herds of zebra and elephant that roam freely between the fringes of the wetlands and the Chobe region to the north.

Camping sites within and on the borders of Moremi are administered by the Botswana Department of Wildlife and National Parks, while several lodges – of both tented camps and permanent (thatched) chalets – are run by private companies. Botswana's official policy, geared to protect the country's fragile ecosystems, encourages high-budget, low-volume tourism, so Moremi (and indeed the country's other sanctuaries) is not really for the back-packer.

Getting Around

The Okavango delta remains a relatively unspoilt wilderness: there are few roads, and the intricate maze of waterways poses a fearsome obstacle to the go-it-alone traveller: apart from its labyrinthine complexity, the con-figuration tends to change with the seasons as the waters find new paths along which to flow, so the delta cannot be mapped in detail.

A wide-ranging tour of this huge area is simply beyond the organisational ability (and pocket) of the average independent tourist, and the majority of visitors make arrangements through one of the numerous safari companies. Most fly you in, at least part of the way (many of the lodges and camps have their own airstrips). If you insist on driving yourself, you'll need a 4x4 as well as confidence in navigating your way along unmarked routes that, in some places, tend to be even less than tracks. Obstacles along the way include patches of deep sand, and fallen trees (pushed over by elephants in their quest for forage). Those routes within the actual delta are restricted to the outer areas of the east and south. Vehicles can be hired at several of the country's centres; Maun is the closest to Okavango.

One of the most restful modes of travel anywhere in the world must surely be a trip by *mokoro*, the dugout craft that is silently and expertly poled along the endless channels by a boatman whose skill and experience make progress seem deceptively easy. The old-style *mokoro*, which carries from three to five people, is carved by adze from the trunk of a hardwood tree such as kiaat. But villagers have been encouraged to use more 'environ-mentally friendly' materials in order to conserve the forests and woodlands, so craft made of glass-reinforced plastic are now common. All the water-based camps and lodges offer guided trips by *mokoro* and also by power-

boat, the latter ranging from small out-boards to elegant cruisers and houseboats. As mentioned, though, you should not attempt to find your own way around, or try to maintain a tight schedule. Channels appear and vanish according to the water level, and although it may be possible to travel by water from, say, Maun to Shakawe, you'll need an expert navigator, a sense of adventure and almost unlimited time to make the journey.

An option that combines both accommodation and travel is the mobile safari, which, in terms of comfort and cost, varies from 'economy' to 'exclusive'. The essence of the mobile safari is flexibility of movement – useful, even essential when following game.

The 'economy' tourists can expect to cater for themselves to some extent, and even to put up with downright discomfort; at the other end of the scale, by contrast, everything is provided from tents to cool drinks, and all is of the highest quality.

Then there is the five-day safari by elephant – a unique (if rather expensive) experience, enjoyed with the co-operation of African elephants repatriated after their working lives in the American circus industry. Apart from the novelty, there's the very real advantage that wild animals usually take little notice of these gentle giants, or of their howdahs and passengers, and your encounters with the wildlife can be memorably close. Elephant safaris are organised from Abu's Camp on the Xhenega River in southwestern Okavango. Horseback safaris are also offered. Based in central Okavango, they too provide a intimate experience of wild Africa. They last from four to 12 days and are best suited to experienced riders.

Visitors with a particular interest, such as environmental study, angling or birdwatching, video-making and photography, can book themselves on outings led by guides with a specialized knowledge of the subject.

Apart from those on Chief's Island, there are no self-guided walking trails in the Okavango – nor, indeed, in any of Botswana's national parks. Conducted trails, though, are routinely offered as part of your *mokoro* excursion, and many private lodges arrange game-spotting walks.

Staying There

The staging post for most visits is the small but rapidly growing town of Maun, situated at the southeastern edge of the delta and reached by an all-tarred road from Gaborone via Francistown. There are several hotels and lodges (offering cottages and camping sites) in the town and surrounding area. The actual delta is also well endowed with lodges and camps (some 50 of them). Those in the Panhandle focus on water activities and bird-watching. The accommodation is invariably attractive, and ranges from tented camps to reed-and-pole huts and thatched dwellings of brick or local stone. The tented camps, despite the images the phrase conjures, can be luxurious: the units are comfortably furnished, often carpeted, and even equipped with hot and cold running water and flush toilets. Each place has its own particular drawcards, but all offer a scenic setting. Many have a raised cocktail bar or observation deck overlooking waterway or floodplain.

Above: Water lilies anchor their roots in the mud of quiet waters while the pads, or leaves, cover much of the still surface.

Below: Sleek and alert, a wild dog keeps watch from the top of a termite mound.

CHOBE NATIONAL PARK

A Marvellous Diversity of Habitats

Location: The park lies in the north-west corner of Botswana.

Climate: May to October are the dry months, during which Savuti, especially, can be bitterly cold at night. September and November, just before the rains, are very hot.

When to go: The park is open throughout the year, but some lodges close between December and February. August to November are the best months for game viewing.

Getting there: Kasane can be reached in little more than an hour's drive from Victoria Falls (Zimbabwe) and from Livingstone (Zambia). The sandy road from Maun is for 4x4 vehicles only (the route is closed during the wet season).

Facilities: Fuel and shops at Kasane; shops at Kachikau and Kavimba in the south; hotels and lodges have all the modern comforts, conveniences and amenities, offering, among other things, boats for hire and/or waterborne safaris; pools, bars and restaurants.

Wildlife: Enormous wintering herds of elephant and buffalo at Savuti provide fine viewing; predators of the many antelope add to the interest; the lions are especially spectacular. Bird life around the northern wetlands is colourful and varied.

Permits and reservations: Entry fees are payable on arrival at the gate. Reservations are not required for camping sites administered by Botswana's Department of Wildlife and National Parks, so these may be crowded. A reputable safari company will handle all the arrangements, well in advance of your intended visit.

Precautions: Against malaria; food should be stored safely away from thieving monkeys, baboons and hyaenas, all of which hover around the fringes of the camps.

Chobe, a huge expanse of game-rich wilderness located in the far north of Botswana, is regarded as one of Africa's finest wildlife sanctuaries. It has everything the ecotourist could wish for, and more: its riverine reaches and their flood-plains echo the splendours of the great Okavango wetlands (see page 136); to the south are grassland plains rolling away to the far horizons; sprawling woodlands and mopane forest and, beyond, the featureless flatness of Kalahari semi-desert enlivened by the occasional natural pan. There is even the bed of a fossil lake, embraced within the vastness of the Mababe depression.

All this, and especially the water-rich northern areas, creates a marvellous diversity of habitats, sustaining the great numbers of elephant, buffalo and antelope for which the Chobe is so renowned, together with the predators that they sustain – lion and leopard, cheetah, wild dog and hyaena. The park's northern limit is delineated by the Linyanti and Chobe rivers – in reality, different sections of the same watercourse – which flow in a generally eastward direction on their way to join the mighty Zambezi. The confluence, near Kasane (the national park's administrative headquarters, even though it lies just beyond the eastern boundary), marks the meeting place of four countries, namely the republics of: Zambia, Namibia, Zimbabwe and, of course, Botswana. Follow the course of the Zambezi River, downstream for an hour or so (the road is negotiable by ordinary family sedan) and you'll get to the Victoria Falls, one the greatest of the world's natural spectacles.

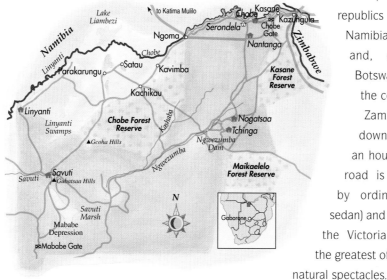

The Northern Rivers

Lesser streams along the Linyanti fan out to create swamplands that are smaller but no less magnificent than those of the Okavango far to the south. Here, in the floodplains and along the banks of the river itself, are the biggest of the game concentrations. The wildlife is prolific, varied – and, in some instances, unusual. Among the wetland area's more distinctive residents are the Chobe bushbuck, a variant species exclusive to this particular corner of Africa; the red lechwe, another rare antelope that is never found far from water, and the even rarer puku, which, again, occurs in the Chobe region and nowhere else. The puku is slightly smaller than the lechwe, with a shoulder height of about 0,8 metres (2 ½ feet) and only the rams carry the small, lyre-shaped

Opposite, top: White-faced duck in flight. These gregarious birds are often seen wading in shallow water.

Opposite, bottom: The puku, one of Africa's rarer antelope, is at the southernmost limit of its range in the Chobe park.

Top right: A Chobe lion in courtship mode.

Above: A traditional fisher-man sets his nets in the waters of the Chobe River.

Below: Elephants enjoy a luxurious wallow.

horns. The animal favours open grass near water, but, curiously, is far less happy on the wide floodplain. Puku cows are notoriously negligent mothers, a failing which the young have countered by becoming self-sufficient at a very early age.

Northern Chobe's 35 kilometres (22 miles) of river frontage, its Lechwe Flats and Puku Flats, are cut through by generally rather rough gravel roads (some are little more than tracks, negotiable only by 4x4) but, for game viewers, and for those that fancy exploring the dense, deep-green riverine forest, they are hugely rewarding. Most of the animals arrive to drink around mid-afternoon, and during the dry winter months one can see elephant aggregations of as many as 300 head. The park as a whole is haven to about 35,000 of these gentle giants – more than is found in any other African

sanctuary. Other highly visible species during this period include buffalo, zebra, the handsome sable, the rare roan, the bushbuck and the tsessebe, an ungainly looking animal but, surprisingly, the swiftest of all antelope.

The swamplands of the Linyanti, upstream from Ngoma, are beautiful, especially in flood time, when the area's resemblance to the Okavango delta is at its most striking. Water channels are lined with papyrus and wild date palm; giant strangler figs grace the riverine forests; woodlands of mopane, acacia and kiaat stretch away to the far horizons. And the water itself is home to hippo and crocodile, bream, barbel, the fighting tigerfish (a favoured catch among sporting anglers) and much else.

River and wetlands are also notable for their abundant bird life. Among some 460 species recorded in the wider park is the white pelican, often seen in groups, the

Above: Graceful impala on the alert on the open plains near Savuti.

Below: Buffalo are highly gregarious, often seen in herds of several hundred within the Chobe park.

South to Savuti

The Mababe Depression, far to the south, was once a lake. But the Savuti Channel, which brought water from the Linyanti some 50 kilometres (30 miles) to the northwest, has now dried up, although there is still the occasional trickle, and some of the overspill from the Okavango delta finds its way south, sometimes to the nearby and somewhat misnamed Savuti Marsh. The 'marsh' is in fact a vast, dry, treeless grassland plain, its pans empty and dusty, coming to life only with the beginning of the wet season in November.

Rain and the greening of the countryside with nutritious grasses heralds the arrival of elephant, buffalo and giraffe, of wildebeest, antelope of various kinds, and of immense herds of zebra, which migrate down from the northern rivers, feeding at Savuti for a few weeks before moving on to the Mababe. All these, in turn, attract the predators and scavengers. Savuti is famed, above all, for its lions, which are numerous, well nourished, and usually at their busiest early in the morning – and at their most visible in winter and spring, when the pans dry out and the prey animals gather in ever-increasing concentrations at the several artificial (borehole-fed) waterholes.

Savuti's Bushman Hill is one of the few places in the Chobe park (apart from the camps and riverside lodges) where you can leave your vehicle. Scramble up the slope and you'll see some fine examples of prehistoric rock art. The paintings are thought to be up to 4,000 years old and show, among readily recognizable objects, animals known to the distant hunter-artists and still found in the area today, including elephant, eland, giraffe, hippo, sable and puff adder.

Above: Reed beds along the Linyanti River provide refuge for water-dependent antelope and an array of bird species.

Right: The strikingly patterned water leguaan is a powerful swimmer, and can also climb trees.

birds trailing one another – effortlessly, it seems, easily holding the air with their three-metre wingspans – in a ragged 'V'-formation strung out across the sky. Colourful little carmine bee-eaters have developed the habit (a localized one, it seems) of riding on the backs of kori bustards. The latter are large birds that stride over the ground in search of prey, and in the process disturb insects that provide an easy meal for their riders. The Chobe's bee-eaters are also unusual in that they normally lay their eggs on the ground rather than, as elsewhere, in tunnels built into sandbanks.

Getting Around

A 4x4 vehicle is essential, although an ordinary sedan may get you from Kasane to Savuti on the main road. Most visitors fly into the region as clients of a safari company, which will handle the travel arrangements and all the other logistics.

Staying There

The Botswana Department of Wildlife and National Parks runs five public camping sites – at Serondela, Linyanti, Savuti, Tshinga and Nogotsaa. The locations are attractive but amenities are minimal, rarely comprising more than showers and toilets. These places are not to be confused with the private camps, which comprise fully and extremely comfortably equipped tents or reed-and-wood chalets. The resort lodges and hotels – of which there are four or five – are magnificently sited, usually with river or wetland views, and for the most part unashamedly luxurious.

Above: A female bushbuck. These shy, usually solitary animals are generally to be found in or near thick riverine vegetation.

Left: King's Pool in the Linyanti River, a favourite wallow for hippo.

THE DESERT PARKS

The Great Spaces of the Kalahari

Newcomers to the splendidly lush wetlands of the Okavango (see page 136) may be surprised to learn that most of Botswana – more than 80 per cent of the land, in fact – is a flat, arid plain where, over countless millennia, wind-blown sand has gradually filled an immense, shallow basin created by ancient movements of the earth's crust.

Botswana lies within the vastness of the Kalahari, a corruption of *kgalagadi* (which means 'great thirst' or 'drying up'). Apart from its northern river system, the region has almost no surface water, but it is rather too well vegetated and receives too much rain to be classed as a true desert. Moreover, it sustains too many wild animals. Indeed this is one of the last of Africa's classic wilderness areas, a land in which the big-game herds remain, for the most part, free to wander across immense tracts of unspoilt countryside.

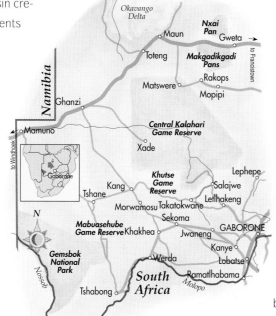

Opposite, top: Palm trees give some shade to a Bushman encampment in the Makgadikgadi area.

Opposite, bottom: Balloon-tyred quad bikes offer an unusual way of exploring the desert countryside.

Top right: A young Bushman girl. The great sandy spaces of the Kalahari are among the last refuges of the traditional clans.

Gemsbok National Park

Two gemsbok parks – South Africa's (see page 98) and Botswana's – occupy the Kalahari's southeastern parts. The latter, 26,000 square kilometres (10,000 square miles) in extent, is separated from its smaller southern counterpart by the dry bed of the Nossob River, though the unfenced boundary is virtually meaningless: two segments are being brought together to form Africa's first transnational or 'Peace Park'. The reddish sands that roll away to the far horizons, the apparent barrenness of the terrain, create an impression of emptiness, but this is an illusion, for there is plenty of life here, and it moves more or less unhindered, sometimes en masse in spectacular migrations, between the two countries.

Springbok are attracted to the short grasses along the riverbeds and the drier pans; gemsbok gravitate towards the taller river grasses that grow after the rains, red hartebeest favour the slightly more wooded areas to the north. Each of these and many other animals has its own preferences, but as food grows scarcer near the riverbed, they all disperse among the dunes. And their predators – lion, cheetah, leopard, spotted hyaena – follow them.

Also present are brown hyaena, Cape and bat-eared fox, three species of mongoose, honey badger (also known as ratel), aardwolf and African wild cat. Occasionally seen is the pangolin or scaly ant-eater, instantly recognisable by its armour-like plates and its

Location: Botswana's desert parks are situated on a northeast/southwest axis, with the Central Kalahari Game Reserve more or less in the centre of the country.

Climate: The rainy season, such as it is, lasts from October to March. Summers are very hot but nights are surprisingly cool. Winter days are pleasantly warm, the nights downright cold.

When to go: The dry season is best for game viewing.

Getting there: Roads are rugged, and although the tarred trans-Kalahari highway is now complete, a 4x4 vehicle is essential for travel within the conservation areas. Air Botswana serves Gaborone and five regional airports, with smaller airlines and charter companies covering the remainder. Most visitors to the parks arrive by air to join an organized safari.

Facilities: These are few and for the most part basic; they do not really extend beyond a number of airstrips and village shops. Water is rarely available at camp sites – or, indeed, anywhere else on the surface – so take your own supplies. All-round self-sufficiency is required when it comes to cooking (by gas or firewood), and vehicles (spare parts and wheels, fuel and accessories).

Wildlife: Botswana not only has the full range of big game (with the exception of rhino), but official policy – low-volume, high-cost tourism – has helped to preserve the environment.

Permits and reservations: Permits are available on entry to national parks. Information is available from the Department of Wildlife and National Parks (see page 174).

Precautions: Approach the great open spaces with caution; plan on complete self-sufficiency.

Right: Baines' Baobabs –
trees that were painted by
the artist and explorer
Thomas Baines in mid-
Victorian times, and little
changed since.

Above: The giant eagle owl,
largest of its family in
southern Africa.

habit, when alarmed, of quickly rolling into a tight ball with its head protected beneath the broad tail. An impressive 265 different kinds of bird, including some grand raptors, have been recorded within the Gemsbok National Park. Busy little sociable weavers – and their massive communal nests – are also prominent.

Most visitors enter the park via Twee Rivieren on the South African side of the border. Farther east, the village of Tshabong can be reached through Botswana in an ordinary vehicle, but after that, you'll need a 4x4.

notably springbok, zebra, wildebeest, hartebeest and eland. It also serves as one of the last natural refuges of the traditional Bushmen or San. However, San numbers are also declining in this area for, among other things, their way of life, and that of the the animals they hunt, is seriously threatened by the fences that are being erected. These artificial barriers are intended to prevent the spread of stock disease rather than to enclose, but their effect on the region's wildlife can be disastrous. For example, more than half a million head of game – wildebeest, hartebeest and zebra – died during one especially severe drought in the 1980s because they were unable to migrate to areas less stricken.

No camping sites have been formally designated, but visitors are free to pitch their tents at suitable spots.

Central Kalahari Game Reserve

This harsh, inhospitable, waterless, hauntingly beautiful expanse of desert terrain is, at 51,800 square kilometres (20, 000 square miles), the world's second-largest conservation area, haven to impressive though dwindling numbers of herbivores and their attendant predators. Most visitors arrive on mobile safaris and, for access, use the airstrip at Deception Pan, where there is a camp. A variety of wildlife can be viewed in the immediate vicinity, and one can embark on game drives to other pans. Central Kalahari is a sanctuary for the migratory herds,

Makgadikgadi and Nxai

The road between Maun and Francistown – now tarred all the way – passes the great pans of Sowa and Ntwetwe which, together, make up the Makgadikgadi complex – vast, shallow, sun-baked depressions whose white, salt-encrusted surfaces assault the eyes with their blinding light. Occasionally, though, they are covered by a thin sheet of water. On the western fringes of the pans lie the Makgadikgadi and Nxai national parks, administered and managed as a single conservation area. The flatness of the plains is not as absolute as it seems: when it rains, innumerable small patches of slightly lower ground are filled to a depth of only a few centimetres, and the waterbirds – pelicans, flamingos and other waterfowl – arrive in their tens of thousands.

A trip to the glaring expanse of the pans can be a solemn reminder that, but for your hardy, all-terrain motor vehicle, you would probably die before ever finding water, and the remoteness and solitude can strike anxiety, even fear into the heart of the first-time visitor. Yet there's reassurance in the tracks of zebra, gemsbok or hartebeest, in sharing with them the same environment. Wildlife includes kudu, wildebeest and other antelope, as well as giraffe, lion, cheetah, hyaena and jackal. There are small numbers of elephant to be found in the north. The mix of riverine and near-desert habitats brings a splendid variety of birds to the pans and their fringes in summer, among them crane, stork, fish eagle, wild goose, teal and a great many waders; ostrich and korhaan stalk the intervening plains.

Visitors have a choice of two public camping sites in the Makgadikgadi section of the park, one at Kumaga and the other at Njuca Hills. Both offer only the very basic of comforts and, if you're bound for Njuca, you have to take your own firewood. The Nxai Pans section also has two camping sites (South Camp and North Camp), both of which are fairly rudimentary although, like almost all such places in Botswana, they do have attractive settings. Comfortable accommodation is available in the villages of Gweta and Nata, which serve as convenient bases for exploring the area.

Above: This bone-dry pan in the Nxai area will occasionally be blessed with a thin sheet of water.

Getting Around

Most visitors to Botswana's desert parks book a package trip in advance, arriving by air to be met by a support team and whisked away in a 4x4.

A hardy minority, however, does the whole journey by land – to say 'by road' would give a misleading impression of this harsh region. The list of even basic essentials is a long one. For the vehicle, it includes a comprehensive tool kit, puncture kit (with spare tubes and a high-lift jack for use on loose ground), engine and electrical spares, spare belts, warning triangles, sand mats, spades, tow rope, extra fuel (and a funnel), spare shock absorbers and spring leaves. Even if you don't know how to fit all these, there's always the chance that a passer-by will be better qualified. You'll also need a full first-aid kit, maps and a compass. It is essential to carry water for drinking and cooking.

Ideally, drivers should have an intimate knowledge of their vehicles and experience of the conditions they will encounter – especially deep sand and mud. 'Charging' a sandy patch is less likely to get you through than approaching slowly and steadily in a low gear with four-wheel drive engaged. Avoid stopping on a pan, but, if you must, check regularly to make sure the vehicle is not slowly breaking through and sinking below the surface crust.

Left: The black-backed jackal is both a resourceful scavenger and a predator, hunting reptiles, insects and the smaller mammals.

ZIMBABWE

Land-locked Zimbabwe, formerly known as Southern Rhodesia and then as the rebel state of Rhodesia until its independence in 1980, is a scenically varied and for the most part beautiful land that occupies some 390,000 square kilometres (150,000 square miles) of south-central Africa's sunlit spaces. The country has common borders with (in clockwise order from the north) Zambia, Mozambique, South Africa and Botswana, plus a tiny stretch shared with Namibia's Caprivi region in the far west; its capital is the attractive little city of Harare; its major tourist attractions include the famed Victoria Falls, the lovely Eastern Highlands, and some of Africa's finest game parks.

The most prominent feature of Zimbabwe's physical make-up is the extensive, elevated region of grassland, some 80 kilometres (50 miles) wide, 1,500 metres (5,000 feet) above sea level and known as the Highveld, that extends across the length of the country from the semi-arid and rather bleak southwest to the grand Nyanga uplands of the northeast. The Highveld is a major watershed, falling away on one side to the valley of the Zambezi and, on the other, to the Limpopo River and the heat-hazed Lowveld.

Although it lies entirely within the tropics, Zimbabwe enjoys a gently temperate climate unspoilt by extremes. The seasons, though, have their distinctive characters: winter (May to August) is a dry period of cold nights and dawns and cloudless, magically warm days. This is followed by a hot, dry two-month spell that heralds the wet season and brings the mopane and other leguminous trees, and the feathery, lilac-coloured jacarandas of the cities, into glorious springtime bloom. The rains proper – torrential late-afternoon downpours – usually start towards the end of November and last until March or April.

Zimbabwe boasts a splendid natural heritage. More than 12 per cent of the country is given over to wildlife conservation, the habitats ranging from the sandy Kalahari grasslands of the Hwange park in the west through the lusher reaches of the Zambezi valley to the heaths and misty montane forests of the eastern uplands.

Left: The glory of a Kariba sunset. The countryside shown here falls within the Matusadona National Park, one of Zimbabwe's finest conservation areas.

Top: An elephant luxuriates in the broad waters of the Zambezi River.

HWANGE NATIONAL PARK

Hunting Ground of the Warrior Kings

It was Mzilikazi, overlord of the Ndebele people of Zimbabwe, who declared an area in the west of his country as his personal hunting preserve, a royal killing ground for the animals that wandered there so abundantly. The boundaries he set are not known, but they overlapped, in part at least, with the present Hwange National Park, a heat-hazed, sandy, 15,000-square kilometre (600-square mile) expanse of bushveld, grassland and woodland between Victoria Falls and the old Ndebele capital of Bulawayo, now Zimbabwe's second largest city.

The great rinderpest epidemic of the later 19th century made savage inroads into southern Africa's wildlife (it also killed some 2.5 million cattle) but the Hwange area staged a steady recovery – a process that accelerated after it was proclaimed a game reserve in 1928. Since then a sustained, scientific conservation programme has restored the herds and their predators to their former abundance, and today the park boasts the greatest density of large animals in Africa, perhaps in the world, though the variety (as opposed to the number) of its species falls short of that of South Africa's Kruger National Park (see page 16).

Forests and Fossils

The central and southern regions of the Hwange park are part – the northeastern segment – of the great Kalahari Desert. Here, deep sands support growths of mopane scrub and a sparse covering of grass. Most of the countryside is flat and sandy: indeed, fossil dunes in the southeastern corner confirm that it was once pure desert. A later, wetter interlude created the ancient riverbeds of which traces can be discerned at Linkwasha Vlei, east of Main Camp, though today streams flow only briefly, when the rains come. Scrubland gives way to forest in the northeast, and here you'll see some of the finest stands of Zimbabwean teak. Mature mopane woodlands cover the broken, hilly country of the northwest.

Creating and sustaining the conservation area (it became a national park in 1950) was a relatively trouble-free exercise because the wilderness, with its poor soils and an inadequate water supply – there are no perennial streams – was unsuited to farming, but more than 45 artificial pans (filled from boreholes) have changed the face of the land and enhanced its wildlife carrying capacity. An intricate network of internal roads

Opposite, top: Elephant cows and calves of a nursery herd pause to drink, shower and wallow.

Opposite, bottom left: Botswana's colourful national bird, the lilac-breasted roller, is equally at home in the Hwange park.

Opposite, bottom centre: A female bateleur displays – stretches her wings – in response to a male's overtures.

Opposite, below right: The crimsonbreasted shrike favours a diet of small prey ranging from insects to nestlings.

Top right: The lovely impala lily produces its succulent leaves in summer, and flowers in winter.

Location: Hwange lies against the Botswana border in the far western part of Zimbabwe

Climate: Hot in summer, sometimes uncomfortably so; warmest month is October. The rainy season lasts from November through to March. Winter days are pleasantly warm.

When to go: At any time of the year, though game viewing is at its best in the cooler, dry months. Elephants tend to migrate across the border in the rainy season.

Getting there: Turn south from the main Victoria Falls–Bulawayo road at the 264.5-km peg and drive 15 km (9 miles) to reach the entrance, which is near Main Camp. Five-day steam safaris from Bulawayo include both the Victoria Falls and Hwange National Park within their itineraries. There are frequent scheduled Air Zimbabwe flights to the park's airfield.

Facilities: Some 500 km (300 miles) of game-viewing roads, with hides and picnic spots, most sited at waterholes. Restaurant, bar, shop and petrol station at Main Camp and Sinamatella. Guided game drives, walks, and wilderness trails (from Robins and Sinamatela) between April and October.

Wildlife: Hwange is one of the best endowed of all African game parks, with a huge elephant population; also impressive numbers of buffalo, giraffe; numerous antelope; lion and other predators; 430 species of bird.

Permits and reservations: Book your accommodation through the Zimbabwe National Parks Central Booking Office (see page 174). Entry permits are available at the gates.

Precautions: Take the standard precautions against malaria.

Right: An inquisitive young giraffe ignores its companion's invitation to a sparring bout of neck-swinging.

Below: The viewing platform at Nyamandhlovu Pan offers unrivalled views of elephant and other big game.

provides access to many of these manmade waterholes, but most of the development has taken place around the main northern visitor centres and the greater part of Hwange remains pristine, its animals virtually undisturbed.

A Place of Elephants

A few kilometres to the south of Main Camp is Nyamandhlovu Pan. Here, especially in the dry season when other water sources have been depleted, you will see one of the most impressive sights of the African wild. The show begins an hour or so before sunset when antelope, interrupted by the arrival of perhaps one or two elephant, ungrudgingly move aside and resume their drinking. A pause, then heads are again raised and turned to the gathering dusk from where, at a brisk, shambling trot, an apparently solid front of elephant makes its appearance. The antelope withdraw; those that are slow to move are simply nudged aside as the herd, numbering between 50 and 100 individuals of both sexes, all ages and sizes, arrives to claim the pan, to drink, wallow and spray muddy water over themselves in a display of sheer delight. They show every sign of enjoyment, but

in fact wallowing is a necessary process, helping the elephant cool its massive bulk. The mud, especially applied over those body areas where the skin is relatively thin, discourages sucking and biting insects and acts as a screen against sunburn.

An adult bull weighing 4.5 tons may drink 250 litres (55 gallons) at a session, and eat more than 200 kilograms (450 pounds) of food daily. Its favourite foods are grasses and reeds, but it is also, perhaps especially, partial to young leaves and tender shoots and may uproot trees to get to those parts that are out of reach. This destructive feeding severely strains the land's ability to sustain such large herds: Hwange is home to close on 30,000 of these giants. The population, though, varies from season to season: during the rains, which fall between November and February or March, they migrate across the border into northern Botswana.

Hwange's wildlife also embraces buffalo, of which the park sustains some 15,000 and which can sometimes be seen in herds of up to 500 and more. There are also giraffe, zebra and numerous types of antelope species in residence. Among the rarer antelope are roan and the elegant sable, both of which carry the ridged, back-swept horns. The sable is the slightly smaller animal; older males have a dark, blackish coat, and females a dark reddish-brown. Both sexes of the roan are a light greyish-brown. Black and white rhino were recently reintroduced, though poachers are a constant threat to their wellbeing. Predators of a different, more orthodox kind, among them lion, leopard and cheetah, are present in healthy numbers. Lion are especially prominent in the vicinity of Robins Camp; smaller carnivores include wild dog, hyaena and the handsome, mainly nocturnal serval (a medium sized cat). An impressive 430 species of bird have been recorded within the park.

Getting Around

Main Camp, just 15 kilometres (nine miles) or so from the Victoria Falls–Bulawayo road, is the start and finish of nine drives thoughtfully planned to give visitors the best chance of seeing as much as possible of Hwange's wildlife. Tour operators offer game-drives based on Main Camp, and you may, of course, use your own vehicle. Apart from the game-viewing roads, there are gravel

Right: A lioness gnaws at the head of its buffalo prey. Lions have no natural enemies, but the mortality rate among the prides is surprisingly high; disease, starvation and male aggression towards the cubs are the main killers.

HWANGE NATIONAL PARK • *Zimbabwe* 159

routes leading to and connecting the various camps, and these too can, for the most part, be negotiated by an ordinary saloon car. A 4x4, though, is advisable if not essential if you're heading for one of the smaller and more secluded camps.

Among the most rewarding excursions from Main Camp is Ten-Mile Drive, which takes at least two hours to complete and includes the well-patronized and rewarding Nyamandhlovu Pan among its waterholes. Also popular, and especially noted for the leopards sometimes seen along the way, is the Lukosi Loop, which starts and finishes at Sinamatela Camp. Some roads, including that to Deka Camp, may be closed during the summer rainy season. Guided walks of about two hours' duration can also be arranged.

Staying There

Largest of the camps are Main and Sinamatella, both easily reached on good roads from the Victoria Falls–Bulawayo road. Each offers one- and two-bedroom cottages, chalets and lodges, together with caravan and camping sites. Less sophisticated but charming in its design and setting is Robins Camp, the third of the major venues. Robins offers chalets with outdoor cooking areas. There are also smaller 'exclusive' camps (for groups) at Bumbusi, Deka, Lukosi and Nantwich. Most of the accommodation has shared cooking facilities, but the lodges are self-contained and fully equipped. Information on all the camps actually within the park, and on visitor facilities generally, may be obtained from the National Parks Central Booking Office.

Hwange Safari Lodge, a luxury hotel situated just outside the park and close to Main Camp, serves as an unofficial gateway, the place where visitors and their guides find one another before entering the park. A magnificent viewing platform overlooks its waterhole. There are also hotels in Hwange town and at Gwai River, and a number of smallish, supremely comfortable, highly individualistic private venues adjacent to the park. Among these are Chokamella, a luxuriously tented camp in a prime game-viewing area; Ivory Lodge, an elegantly rustic venue which offers the classic African experience. Jabulisa, a graciously converted old farmstead, Kanondo (tree houses), Makalolo (luxury tents), Sable Valley (which hosted Queen Elizabeth and Prince Philip in 1990), and Sikumi (tree houses).

Opposite, top: The tree squirrel is an alert forager on the ground, where it feeds on roots and insects. It makes its nest, however, in a tree.

Opposite, bottom: A white rhino cow, its calf and a group of impala antelope seem undisturbed by the presence of humans on horseback.

Left: The heavily horned head and unblinking stare of the African buffalo at close range, is a sight dreaded by old-time hunters.

Left: As inquisitive as human children, young chacma baboons scramble up to an adult male that sits atop a termite mound.

THE ZAMBEZI RIVER

From the Thunder of the Victoria Falls to the

Limpid Pools of Mana

Location: Northwestern Zimbabwe

Climate: Summers are usually very hot; winter days are pleasantly cool but nights can be cold. The rainy season lasts from end October or November to March or April.

When to go: The river at the Victoria Falls reaches peak flow from February to April. Game viewing, especially at Mana Pools, is best in the dry (winter and spring) season.

Getting there: Victoria Falls is accessible by train, road and air; Kariba by road and air; Mana Pools by road (it also has an airstrip for non-scheduled flights).

Facilities: Victoria Falls offers hotels, casinos, restaurants, shops, banks, service stations. Canoes, kayaks, 4x4 vehicles available for hire. Among the more exhilerating activities are white-water rafting and bungee-jumping (from the Victoria Falls bridge). Sightseeing options include trips by air (helicopter and fixed wing), sunset cruises, game drives. The traditional craft village and the crocodile farm are prominent attractions. Lake Kariba offers excellent hotels and safari lodges, a casino; cruisers, houseboats and pontoons for hire; game walks and drives; splendid opportunities for angling (for bream and tigerfish). Mana Pools has game-viewing roads, camp sites and private lodges.

Wildlife: The Kariba area and Mana Park are renowned for their big game animals.

Landscapes: Victoria Falls is one the world's scenic wonders.

Permits and reservations: For accommodation or a camping site in the various national parks, contact the National Parks Central Booking Office (see page 174).

Precautions: Malaria; bilharzia.

The Zambezi, Africa's fourth-largest river (after the Nile, the Congo and the Niger), cuts a majestic course of some 2,700 kilometres (1,700 miles) from its source in northwest Zambia to the Indian Ocean in the east. It is a magnificent watercourse, flanked in places by the deep-green of woodland and lush riverine forest, in others by wetland plain, huge in flood, placid enough and even sluggish in its broader reaches but whipped to a tumultuous, white-foamed frenzy when it negotiates its falls, rapids and ravines.

The Zambezi's great dams – Kariba in Zimbabwe and Cahora Bassa in Mozambique – have drawn international attention to the river, but not nearly as sensationally as it was brought to world notice in 1855, when missionary and explorer David Livingstone provided the first published account of 'the smoke that thunders': the

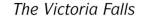

Victoria Falls, one of the most awe-inspiring wonders of the natural world. The scene, Livingstone wrote, 'must have been gazed upon by angels in their flight.'

Today, the falls are just one (though undoubtedly the most spectacular) destination among many on the course of a mighty river.

The Victoria Falls

Here you will find the largest curtain of falling water on earth: the first of the five immense cataracts, fully 106 metres (348 feet) high and 1,786 metres (5,858 feet) wide, is twice as lofty as Niagara and one and a half times broader. At peak flood, in April and May, over 600 million litres (132 million cubic gallons) of water cascade over the rim each minute, and the roar is audible 20 kilometres (about 12 miles) away, the rising cloud of mist discernible from 80 kilometres (50 miles). On closer view, you will see rainbows painted on the wall of spray, creating ethereally lovely images in the midst of noise and raw power.

Having negotiated the falls, the torrent churns and tumbles in the chasm called The Boiling Pot and then races into a narrow, winding canyon that extends for for more than 70 kilometres (44 miles), the waves and whirlpools presenting one of the stiffest of challenges to river-boaters anywhere.

The cataracts are the focus of the Victoria Falls National Park, a narrow expanse of riverbank and backing countryside created to preserve both the spectacle

Opposite, top: The main cataract of the Victoria Falls, seen here in early morning, create a curtained amphitheatre in the massive, water-worn gorge.

Opposite, centre: Cattle egret follow in the footsteps of elephant in the Mana Pools park, feeding on the insects disturbed by the animals' passage.

Opposite, bottom: Luxury cruisers ply Lake Kariba, under whose quiet surface the waters of the Zambezi River still flow along their ancient channels.

Top right: Adventure-seekers, riding their inflatable raft, challenge the waters of the gorge below Victoria Falls.

Above: An intrepid bungee jumper launches out from the high railway bridge that spans the river, near the Victoria Falls.

and its adjoining rainforest, a magical sanctuary for birds and butterflies, for fig, ebony, mahogany and sausage trees, palms, ferns, orchids, vines, lianas and a tangled, dripping mass of other creepers and climbers, the whole nurtured to a fecund richness by the ever-present spray and the humus of the soil. Some of the park's plants are extremely rare; the fern *Cheilanthes farinosa* occurs in only one other place. The rainforest is also haven for bushbuck, vervet monkey and warthog; notable among the birds of the adjacent gorges are black eagle and the rare, endemic Taita falcon (*Falco fasciinucha*). The path that leads through the trees takes you to the very edge of the canyon, where there is an observation platform.

There's plenty to see and do at and around the Victoria Falls. The village itself is a bustling little place with all the amenities – shops, banks, service stations, tour and transport facilities (cars, scooters and bicycles can be hired) and, here and in the immediate area, restaurants, top-grade hotels, casinos, and a busy international airport.

Apart from taking in the sights and sounds, visitors – the braver ones – can bungee jump from the historic river bridge (it links Zimbabwe with neighbouring Zambia) or ride the white waters downriver on a canoe or, more usually, a raft; embark on the popular sunset cruise upriver, or on a rather less sociable but perhaps more satisfying fishing cruise; take to the air on the short 'Flight of Angels' sightseeing excursion; visit the snake park, the crocodile ranch (5,000 of these giant reptiles are in residence) and, most especially, the multicultural craft village, which is renowned for its displays of traditional music, dancing, ornamentation and lifestyles.

Along the south bank of the river just upstream from the falls is the Zambesi National Park, an attractive, 56,000-hectare (220-square mile) sanctuary for a variety of game big and small. Zambezi Drive, which starts at the falls and follows the riverbank, takes you though thickly vegetated riverine countryside to some enchanting fishing spots and picnic sites. Beware crocodile and hippo. On Chamabondo Drive, the southern game viewing route, there's a good chance of seeing sable, waterbuck, buffalo, kudu, zebra, elephant and, if you're lucky, lion, leopard and cheetah. Visitors can overnight at one or other of the park's two six-bed lodges and five exclusive camps (each designed for party of up to 12). The fairly basic fishing camps can accommodate ten people at a time.

Right: A fine mist rises from the tumultuous waters during the months of high flow.

Opposite: The Zambezi, in full flood, thunders into the turbulent, spray-draped mouth of the gorge.

Above: A quiet moment on the lake's shore. Kariba's waters are usually placid, but not always so: occasional, sudden windstorms whip up large waves.

Below: Relic of an immensely distant past, this fossil tooth plate, which belonged to a primitive lungfish, was found in the Matusadona park.

The Great Lake

At Kariba, some 450 kilometres (280 miles) downstream from Victoria Falls, the broad reaches of the Zambezi have been dammed to form a vast reservoir, almost an inland sea, that stretches for 280 kilometres (175 miles), covers more than 5,000 square kilometres (1,930 square miles) of what was once dry bushveld, and in places reaches a depth of no less that 116 metres (380 feet). When it was completed in 1958, it ranked as the world's largest manmade lake.

The rising waters transformed the region's human geography: during the 1950s some 50,000 indigenous people of the Tonga group were relocated; in due course busy (and economically important) fishing villages were born and grew along the lakeshore.

The dam provides a stable basis for a number of wildlife habitats that include the water itself, the shoreline, the islands, and the fjord-like estuaries that are in reality remnants of half-drowned hills and valleys. Plants and animals have adapted to the annual fluctuations of the water level, and indeed have derived huge benefit from them: elephant and buffalo, giraffe and a host of other animals are drawn in great numbers to the the nutritious vegetation – a mix of aquatic and terrestial grasses – that lies between the tide lines. Life in the lake itself, nurtured by the dead vegetation of drowned forests, includes some 42 species of fish, among them them fat bream, the spirited tigerfish (much sought after by the sporting angler) and kapenta, a small, protein-rich, sardine-like species caught in great quantities by the local

villagers. Close by the dam wall is the town of Kariba, an attractive little centre noted for, among other things, its unusual church – an open-walled, circular building of archways and bright murals, and for the nearby crocodile farm, where there is fine leatherwork on display.

Kariba caters expertly for visitors: the hotels that fringe the lake offer comfortable accommodation, lovely vistas and plenty of recreational facilities, including boat hire, sightseeing packages and game-viewing excursions. One can also live on the water itself: well-equipped houseboats and cruisers are available for hire. These craft vary greatly in size and design, ranging from the small and functional to the large and luxurious.

Most of those intent on exploring the lake hire a craft of one sort or another, or join a conducted tour. A pleasant alternative, though, is to take the public ferry which regularly plies the 280 kilometres (175 miles) between Andora harbour, close to Kariba village, and Mlibizi at the western end. The vessels have pleasantly appointed saloons (there are no cabins), the food is good, and there are full bar facilities on board. The views from deck, of both landscapes and lakeshore wildlife, are memorable.

Kariba's Wildlife Sanctuaries

Best known and most visited of the region's three splendid conservation areas is Matusadona National Park, an extensive (1,500-square kiolometre/580-square mile) expanse of rugged Zambezi escarpment countryside at the lake's eastern end. The park is bounded in the north by the lakeshore, an aquatic

wilderness of bays and beaches, inlets, offshore islands and river estuaries that shrink and grow with the rise and fall of the water.

The great spaces are hilly, grand in their vistas, covered in bush and mixed woodland featuring bush willow, lovely msasa trees and commiphora (also known as *kanniedood* or 'never die'). Hippo and crocodile are probably the most visible of the park's residents, but elephant and buffalo, a range of large antelope, zebra, lion and spotted hyaena are also prominent. Bird life is rich, and at its most varied along the shore.

Matusadona has three exclusive rest camps that offer two-bedroomed family units to parties of up to ten guests at a time, and camping sites at Tashinga and Sanyati West (equipment can be hired at both places). For those who like their comforts, luxury accommodation is available at the Bumi Hills Safari Lodge, on the western edge of the park. The roads that lead to Matusadona are not recommended, whatever the season, but the park is easily accessible by boat from Kariba village, and by light aircraft. Within the park are a few rough tracks, which are closed off during the rainy season, and a network of wilderness trails.

Situated close to Kariba village is the Charara Safari Area, an equally pristine swathe of hill and woodland countryside that also hosts a splendid complement of wild animals. Among especially rewarding vantage points are the elevated platform and strategically sited picnic spots, developed by the Wildlife Society of Zimbabwe, around the lakeshore. Camping and caravan sites are available at Nyanyana, something of a gathering place for the thirsty wildlife (elephants have been known to wander through the camp itself).

The third of the Kariba region's major protected areas is Chizarira National Park, a remote, barely penetrable, 200,000-hectare (770-square mile) sprawl of mountainous terrain that rises to a peak called Tundazi – which is the home, according to local legend, of an immense snake endowed with awesome powers. Chizarira lies on the edge of the great central plateau some 50 kilometres (30 miles) to the south of Kariba, and is famed for the wild beauty of its landscapes: the escarpment falls steeply through some 600 metres (2,000 feet) towards the Zambezi valley and its great lake, and the views from the top are memorable indeed. In springtime the hills are decorated with wild flowers.

Chizarira's southern boundary is marked by the course of the Busi River and its floodplains, a riverine strip dense with stately ana trees (*Acacia albida*). The central areas are distinguished by rolling plains crisscrossed by hilly ridges and ranges and deep-cut river gorges – the kind of terrain that resists man's encroachment and thus serves as an ideal refuge for elephant, buffalo, zebra, antelope and their attendant predators. The game-viewing routes are negotiable only by 4x4 vehicles. Other options include a conducted wilderness trail of up to ten days' duration, and guided game drives.

Manzituba, in the west, has an airstrip and functions as Chizarira's headquarters. There are several basic camps, of which only one – Kaswiswi – boasts hot water and waterborne sewerage. A pleasant alternative is the privately run Chizarira Wilderness Lodge, a charming cluster of tree-shaded chalets, comfortably appointed and scenically sited high up on the escarpment.

Above: Buffalo graze beneath the skeletal remains of dead trees in Matusadona, a game-rich area flanking Lake Kariba's southern shore.

Below: Among the wild kingdom's most enduring life forms is the Nile crocodile: it has survived virtually unchanged in form from the days of the dinosaurs.

Above: The attractive little carmine bee-eater extends its foraging range by perching on the back of larger birds – among them ostriches, storks and cranes – as they stalk about in search of their own food.

Right: A guide regales trailists with tales of the baobab, a bizarre tree around which many African legends have been woven.

Right: Canoeists at placid Mana Pools, on the wide course of the Zambezi, set off on waters that are a fisherman's dream: they are home to barbel, bream, vundu, tigerfish and other species. Crocodile and hippo, however, discourage bathing.

Mana Pools National Park

To the northeast of Lake Kariba is one of the last of Africa's true wilderness areas. The Zambezi first flows north and then loops around to the west to meander across the plains, and over the centuries its sluggish floodwaters have left behind rich deposits of alluvial soil which support grasses, acacia and mopane. The river's convoluted course has also created shallow depressions and channels in which water collects and remains, even in the long dry season.

The moisture and the nutritious vegetation attract wildlife in huge numbers to these, the middle reaches of the great Zambezi: in the hot, dry weeks just before the onset of the summer rains in November the animals, parched and hungry, come down in their thousands from the high escarpment country to feast on the lush grazing of the riverine terraces. Great herds of elephant – they total around 12,000 animals (the highest concentration in the world) – gather on the plains, to be joined by

enormous concourses of buffalo, zebra and antelope of many kinds, including the rare nyala. Lion, leopard, cheetah, hyaena and wild dog gather for easy pickings; baboons are everywhere to be seen. And always, of course, there are hippos and crocodiles. Birdlife, a mix of forest and water species, is both abundant and attractive.

Mana Pools National Park, which has a 70-kilometre (45-mile) river frontage, caters for both overnighters and day visitors. There is permanent accommodation in two pleasant riverside lodges (self-catering eight-bed units); Nyamepi, the main caravan-camping ground; three rather remote campsites (for groups), and the Nyamuomba fishing camp. The fishing – notably for bream, vundu and tigerfish – is excellent. There are trail paths and a network of game viewing roads, which are rather rough but can be negotiated by ordinary saloon car, though a 4x4 is preferable. The number of day-visitor vehicles allowed in the park is limited; enquire about access before setting out.

Above: A square-ended tail, red throat and white forehead are distinctive features of the white-fronted bee-eater, often observed along dry river-courses.

Left: Opportunistic elephant at Mana Pools help them-selves to fruits gathered, and then dropped, by over-burdened baboons.

Left: Mother and child: Burchell's zebra in the Mana Pools area. These equine animals are distin-guished by their shadow stripes, though no two individuals have exactly the same pattern.

THE EASTERN HIGHLANDS

The Green and Pleasant Land

For sheer scenic beauty, few regions of southern African can compare with the series of hills and high mountains that runs for 300 kilometres (about 180 miles) along the edge of Zimbabwe's central plateau, demarcating the country's eastern border area before the land descends, precipitously in some places, to the steamy lowlands of neighbouring Mozambique. The countryside is well wooded, emerald green in all its seasons, ranging from the rolling downlands of Nyanga in the north to the imposing quartzitic cliffs of the Chimanimani mountains in the south. Much of the region lies between 2,000 and 2,300 metres (6,500 and 7,500 feet) above sea level; its highest point is Mount Inyangani, which rises to 2,592 metres (8,508 feet).

The Eastern Highlands are a popular resort area, and deservedly so: the landscapes are a visual delight; trout streams beckon the sporting angler, and the cool, clean air of the misty mountains provides welcome relief from the summer heat of Zimbabwe's lower-lying parts.

Opposite: A springtime ocean of massed msasa trees mantles the hills of the Nyanga National Park, the colours of their leaves ranging from bronze to red, yellow and green.

Top right: The 'Chimanimani pin-cushion', a protea which forms a compact shrub, was thought to be endemic to the Eastern Highlands but has recently been found growing far to the south, in the South African Drakensberg.

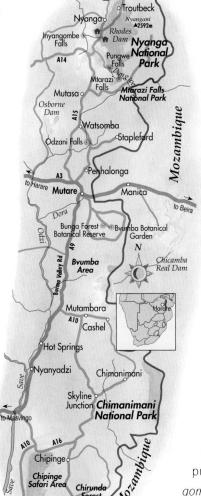

The region's principal urban centre is the attractive little city of Mutare, located some 100 kilometres (60 miles) south of Nyanga National Park and north of the Bvumba, the 'mountains of mist' which embrace, among much else of enchantment and interest, the Bunga Forest Reserve and the Bvumba Botanical Gardens. Farther south are the Chimanimanis, Zimbabwe's biggest and most impressive mountain range and part of a wider conservation area that ends at Chirinda Forest Reserve. The latter is noted for the pockets of rare primeval forest that still clothe its deeper ravines.

The Nyanga Park

Mount Inyangani, at the northern end of the Eastern Highlands, dominates the 47,000-hectare (180-square mile) park, a well-watered expanse of peak and plain punctuated here and there by *gomos*, imposing outcrops of smooth, dome-like rock. Although many of the slopes are under plantations of pine, there are enough indigenous trees of various types to create magnificent displays of colour, hues that range from gold to crimson, in springtime. Chief of these is the handsome msasa. The area's rich flora also includes the endemic *Aloe inyangensis*, found at the higher, cooler altitudes.

Location: The Eastern Highlands extend both north and south of the city of Mutare, which lies 260 km (160 miles) southeast of Harare, the country's capital.

Climate: Temperate; rarely uncomfortable. October is the hottest month (as it is throughout the country), May the coolest. Winter nights can be cold. The wider region's rainy season runs from November through to March, but mist and rain may occur at almost any time in the uplands.

When to go: At any time of the year. The msasa trees come into flower in spring, making an attractive show. The parks are open daily.

Getting there: Nyanga and the Bvumba are accessible by tarred road from Mutare. Chimanimani, which lies further south, is accessible off a gravel road that may be difficult to negotiate after rain.

Facilities: The Nyanga and Bvumba areas offer scenic drives; picnic sites; good hotels (angling; golf; swimming pools; guided pony trails). Nyanga is famous for its trout-stocked dams.

Activities: Scenic drives; walks; pony trails, trout-fishing; golf.

Landscapes: Mountain and forest. The views are superlative, both in the reserves and along the roads between them.

Wildlife: The Eastern Highlands are known for the number and variety of their birds. Several antelope species are to be seen; leopard and smaller mammals are present but elusive.

Permits and reservations: Entry permits are obtainable at the gates to the reserves. Accommodation may be booked through the Zimbabwe National Parks Central Booking Office (see page 174).

The park is especially renowned for its crystal, trout-filled streams and its waterfalls, among them those of the Pungwe, largest of the region's rivers. The falls thunder over the lip of the escarpment to plunge 240 metres (790 feet) into the long, densely wooded Pungwe Gorge. Not quite so dramatic but just as lovely are the nearby Mtarazi Falls, a thin, silvery ribbon of water that drops a full 760 metres (2,500 feet), in two stages, over granite cliffs and into the rainforest of the Honde River valley.

Nyanga is principally a scenic park but it does have its wildlife, numbering among its larger species the kudu and wildebeest, waterbuck, reedbuck, duiker and samango monkey. Bird life is prolific; notable are the rare marsh tchagra and the appealing Narina trogon, a brilliantly coloured resident of the forest patches.

Nyanga and Mutare are linked by a tarred road, and the park is criss-crossed by a number of gravel-surfaced routes that lead you to viewpoints, to the dams and waterfalls and to some of the ancient stone structures — sunken enclosures, cattle pens, forts and terraced retaining walls — built by the region's long-gone Iron Age communities. Perhaps the most memorable of the vistas unfolds from World's View, which overlooks an immen-

Above: Dense woodland embraces the long plunge of the Pungwe River.

Below: Fly-fishing is one of the major attractions of the Eastern Highlands.

Right: Foliage-filtered sunlight creates dappled patterns on a road through the Bunga Forest Botanical Reserve near Mutare.

sity of countryside to the west. A well-marked footpath leads to the summit of Mount Inyangani, from where there are also superlative views.

The Bvumba: Flowers and Forest

A round trip of less than 80 kilometres (50 miles) from Mutare, on tarred roads, will enable you to take in much of what the Bvumba has to offer. This hilly land – set high above the tropical Burma Valley and its ordered plantations of banana and mango, tea and tobacco, coffee and cotton – is cool, often misty, a magical place of flowers, ferns and forest. The Bunga Forest Botanical Reserve, which sustains a wealth of indigenous evergreen trees, enjoys its own mini-climate, an environment created by altitude and by its position on a cliff edge, where rising currents of air cool and condense. Samango monkeys, birds and butterflies are much in evidence; shy duiker and civet are present but rarely seen by day. Apart from the footpaths that lead to viewsites and waterfalls, the quiet countryside remains wholly undisturbed.

Within a few kilometres of the Bunga forest is the Bvumba Botanical Garden, graced for the most part by indigenous trees but partly given over to a spacious garden cultivated in English-country style, its ponds, streams, pathways and footbridges surrounded by a riot of such exotics as azaleas, roses, and fuchsias. The massed displays of blooms are quite breathtaking. African plants (including ferns and ancient cycads) also feature, and the herb garden illustrates the many uses to which the various plant families have been put, both locally and abroad.

Chimanimani National Park

Perennial streams have cut deep gorges across this high-lying, wild, forested and lovely country of craggy outcrops, lichen-daubed granite cliffs and high peaks, of cedars and yellowoods, everlastings, proteas and arum lilies, and of deep forest in whose moist shadows ferns, mosses and orchids thrive. The Chimanimani park – which extends across about a third of the mountain range; the remainder is within Mozambique territory – is also distinguished by its waterfalls, some of them of quite exquisite delicacy. Particularly notable is the Bridal Veil. Wildlife includes eland, sable, bushbuck and duiker, and a splendid array of birds, including some fine raptors. Leopards, although present, rarely allow themselves to be seen.

There are no roads in the Chimanimani. One explores the uplands on foot; recommended is the three-hour Bailey's Folly Walk, which starts and ends at Mutekeswane. Here the Department of National Parks maintains a base camp, and an information office where you can find out about (among much else) camping sites. Bailey's Folly is just one of a myriad choices available to the walking enthusiast.

Staying There

Accommodation within Nyanga National Park includes two-, five- and eight-bed lodges and two camping and caravan sites. There are several hotels in the area, the most notable perhaps the luxurious (though unpretentious) Troutbeck Inn, which has its own trout-filled lake and golf course. Supplies and fuel may be bought at Nyanga village.

The Bvumba is also well served by hotels, among them the cosy White Horse Inn; the Inn of the Bvumba and, perhaps the best known, the castle-like Leopard Rock. A restaurant at the Bvumba nursery section serves refreshments.

Chimanimani has a rudimentary communal hut and, at the base camp, a small camping site (no caravans). There is a hotel in Chimanimani village.

Getting Around

Clearly marked footpaths enable visitors to explore the three different areas at will. Roads in the Nyanga and Bvumba uplands are both well maintained and marvellously scenic, easily negotiated by family car although travellers could, occasionally, encounter problems after heavy rain.

Left: Chimanimani's aptly named Bridal Veil Falls drop 50 metres (162 feet), the water descending in gentle cascades between a dense growth of ferns and trees.

Below: The rugged heights of the Chimanimani mountains – a mecca for the hiker, and for the lover of wild flowers.

USEFUL ADDRESSES

SOUTH AFRICA:

South African National Parks

P.O. Box 787, Pretoria 0001

Tel: (012) 343 1991, Fax: (012) 343 0906

Cape Town: P.O. Box 7400, Roggebaai 8012

Tel: (021) 422 2810, Fax: (021) 424 6211

Satour (South African Tourism Board)

Private Bag X164, Pretoria 0001

Tel (012) 347 0600, Fax: (012) 347 8753

KwaZulu-Natal Nature Conservation Service

P.O. Box 13069, Cascade, Pietermaritzburg 3202

Tel: (0331) 845 1000, Fax: (0331) 845 1001

Eastern Cape Nature Conservation

Private Bag X5001, Greenacres, Port Elizabeth 6057

Tel: (041) 373 8891, Fax: (041) 373 7118

Western Cape Nature Conservation

Private Bag X9086, Cape Town 8000

Tel: (021) 483 4051/4615, Fax: (021) 483 3713

Northern Cape Province Nature Conservation Service

Private Bag X6102, Kimberley 8300

Tel: (053) 832 2143, Fax: (053) 831 3530

NAMIBIA:

Namibian Wildlife Resorts

Private Bag X13267, Windhoek

Tel/fax: (61) 224 900

Namibian Tourism, Cape Town, tel: (021) 419 3190

Namibian Tourism, Johannesburg, tel: (011) 622 1669

BOTSWANA:

Department of Wildlife and National Parks

P.O. Box 131, Gaberone

Tel: 580 774, Fax: 580 775

Parks and Reservations Office

P.O. Box 20364, Maun

Tel: 661 265, Fax: 308 675

Department of Tourism

Tel: 353 024, Fax: 308 675

ZIMBABWE:

National Parks Central Booking Office

Department of National Parks and Wildlife Management

P.O. Box 8151, Causeway, Harare

Tel: (4) 706 077, Fax: (4) 724 914

Zimbabwe Tourism Authority

P.O. Box CY 286, Causeway, Harare

Tel: (4) 706 077, Fax: (4) 758 828

FURTHER READING

Balfour, D., Balfour, S. and Joyce, P. (1994) *This is Botswana*. Struik Publishers, Cape Town.

Bannister, A. and Ryan, B. (1993) *National Parks of South Africa*. Struik Publishers, Cape Town.

Comley, P. and Meyer, S. (1994) *Traveller's Guide to Botswana*. New Holland Publishers, London and Cape Town.

Cubitt, G. and Joyce, P. (1992) *This is Namibia*. Struik Publishers, Cape Town.

Ginn, P.J., McIlleron, W.G., and Milstein, P. le S. (1989) *The Complete Book of Southern African Birds*. Struik Winchester, Cape Town.

Levy, J. (1993) *The Complete Guide to Walks and Trails in Southern Africa*. Struik Publishers, Cape Town.

Mills, G. and Hes, L. (1997) *The Complete Book of Southern African Mammals*. Struik Publishers, Cape Town.

Reader's Digest (1992) *The Great South African Outdoors*. Reader's Digest Association, Cape Town.

Sinclair, I. and Hockey, P. (1996) *SASOL: The Larger Illustrated Guide to the Birds of Southern Africa*. Struik Publishers, Cape Town.

Skinner, J. and Smithers, R.H.N. (1990) *The Mammals of the Southern African Subregion*. University of Pretoria, Pretoria.

Stuart, C. and Stuart, T. (1995) *Africa: A Natural History*. Southern Book Publishers, Johannesburg.

Stuart, C. and Stuart, T. (1997) *Guide to Southern African Game & Nature Reserves*. Struik Publishers, Cape Town.

Stuart, C. and Stuart, T. (1996) *Africa's Vanishing Wildlife*. Southern Book Publishers, Johannesburg.

Van Wyk, B. and Van Wyk, P. (1997) *Field Guide to Trees of Southern Africa*. Struik Publishers, Cape Town.

Walker, C. (1991) *Signs of the Wild*. Struik Publishers, Cape Town.

Picture Credits

Abbreviations: PAPL = Photo Access Photographic Library; SIL = Struik Image Library. Photographic credits read from top to bottom, and from left to right. **Adrian Bailey:** 12a, 136, 141b, 142b, 143b, 145. **Daryl Balfour:** 124b, 128b/129b. **Pat de la Harpe:** 36d, 41b, 50b. **Roger de la Harpe:** 2/3, 8, 9, 10, 11, 12b, 15, 28, 29, 30a-c, 31a-c, 32a-c, 33, 34, 35, 36a-c, 37b, 38, 40a-d, 41a, 42b, 43a-c, 44a&b, 45a-c, 46, 47, 48a-c, 49a&b, 50a, 51, 52a-c, 53, 54a-d, 55, 58, 59, 60a&b, 61a&b, 62a-c, 65a, 68a&c, 69, 70a&b, 72a&b, 76b, 77, 78, 79c&d, 80a&b, 81c, 82a/83a, 82b, 83b, 84b, 86b, 87a, 88, 89, 90b, 91a, 92a, c&d, 93, 97a, 104c, 106, 107, 109, 110c, 111a&b, 112a&d, 113, 114a, 115c, 116, 118b&c, 119b, 120a&b, 121, 129a, 143a, 151, 154, 155, 155b, 156a-d, 157, 158a&b, 159, 160a&b, 161a&b, 162b&c, 164a&b, 165, 166a&b, 167a&b, 168a-c, 169a-c, 170, 171, 172a, 173a&b. **Nigel Dennis:** 1, 5, 6, 13b, 14, 16a&c, 17, 18a&b, 19a-c, 20/21, 22a&b, 23a&b, 24a-c, 25a, 26a&b, 27a&b, 37a, 42a, 56, 57, 64a, 65c, 66a-d, 67, 68b, 73a&b, 74, 75, 76a&c, 79a&b, 81a&b, 86a&c, 87b, 90a, 92b, 94, 95, 97b&c, 98a-c, 99, 100a-d, 101a&b, 102a-d, 103, 104a&b, 105a&b, 108, 110a&b, 112b&c, 114b, 115a&b, 117, 118a, 119a, 122a&b, 124a, 125a&b, 126/127, 128a, 142a. **Jean du Plessis:** 131, 132a&b, 133b. **Richard du Toit:** 122c, 135, 139a&b, 140a&c, 141a, 144a&b, 146a&b, 147a&b, 148b, 149a. **Gallo Images/Roger de la Harpe:** 39, 41c, 71, 152a. **Gwynneth Glass:** 85. **Martin Harvey:** 134, 138c. **J & B Photographers:** 63, 64b, 65b&d. **Peter Lawson:** 130a, 130b, 133a. **Ian Michler:** 137, 138b. **PAPL/C.F.Bartlett:** 148a. **PAPL/Getaway/ D.Bristow:** 149b. **PAPL/Vanessa Burger:** 153a. **PAPL/Getaway/J.Nel:** 150a&b. **PAPL/Getaway/D.Steele:** 138a, 140b. **PAPL/Getaway/ P.Wagner:** 153b. **Pippa Parker:** 123. **SIL:** 84a, 172c. **SIL/Nigel Dennis:** 152b. **SIL/Roger de la Harpe:** 162a. **SIL/Peter Pickford:** 172b. **SIL/Mark Skinner:** 163. **SIL/Lanz von Hörsten: Mark Skinner:** 96.16b. **Hein von Hörsten:** 91b.